THE BAFFLED PARENT'S GUIDE TO

TEACHING KIDS
GOL.

D0118310

Look for these other Baffled Parent's Guides by Ragged Mountain Press

The Baffled Parent's Guide to Coaching Youth Baseball,
by Bill Thurston

The Baffled Parent's Guide to Coaching Youth Basketball,
by David G. Faucher

The Baffled Parent's Guide to Coaching Youth Soccer,
by Bobby Clark

The Baffled Parent's Guide to Coaching Youth Softball,
by Jacquie Joseph

THE BAFFLED PARENT'S
GUIDE TO
TEACHING KIDS
GOLF

Betty Moore

LPGA Class A Teaching Professional

Ragged Mountain Press/McGraw-Hill

Camden, Maine • New York • Chicago • San Francisco • Lisbon
London • Madrid • Mexico City • Milan • New Delhi • San Juan
Seoul • Singapore • Sydney • Toronto

Ragged Mountain Press
A Division of The **McGraw·Hill** *Companies*

10 9 8 7 6 5 4 3 2 1

Library of Congress Cataloging-in-Publication Data
Moore, Detty.
  The baffled parent's guide to teaching kids golf / Bernadette Moore
     p.   cm.
Includes index.
   ISBN 0-07-137025-0 (alk. paper)
   1. Golf for children—Study and Teaching. I. Title.

GV966.3.M66 2001
796.352´0 7´7 —dc21   2001001786

Questions regarding the content of this book should be addressed to
Ragged Mountain Press
P.O. Box 220
Camden, ME 04843
www.raggedmountainpress.com

Questions regarding the ordering of this book should be addressed to
The McGraw-Hill Companies
Customer Service Department
P.O. Box 547
Blacklick, OH 43004
Retail customers: 1-800-262-4729
Bookstores: 1-800-722-4726

This book is printed on 70-lb. Citation by Quebecor World, Fairfield, PA
Design by Carol Gillette
Illustrations by Accurate Art
Illustration on page 14 by Kerry Gross
Photography by Allen Pearson, except where otherwise noted
Production by Eugenie S. Delaney and Dan Kirchoff
Edited by Tom McCarthy and Cynthia Flanagan Goss

Cayman and Surlyn are registered trademarks.

*I would like to dedicate this book with love and gratitude
to my family on both sides of the Atlantic.*

Contents

Foreword

As director of one of Florida's busiest municipal golf facilities, I see count-less numbers of struggling golfers of all ages. Our juniors are no exception. Almost every day I see anxious parents "helping" their youngsters. Many times they are indeed helping, but often by accident as much as by plan or purpose.

What a wonderful contribution Detty Moore is making toward solving that situation with this book! Now, not only can parents help their young-sters get into golf early in life: they can also do it with guidance and confi-dence, knowing they're going about it in a way that is productive and enjoyable for their child.

I know of no one more qualified to create this guiding light for par-ents than Detty Moore. I first met her when she was completing her gradu-ate degree requirements by working at the National Golf Foundation. It quickly became evident that her first love was educating children, and that was followed closely by her second love, golf. This book not only allows her to combine those two loves but to expand her influence and share the wealth of knowledge and professional wisdom she has gained throughout her years in education and as an LPGA professional.

I believe this book will become standard equipment for parents and volunteer coaches of juniors. It is full of useful, practical advice based on research in child development on how children learn best. And you don't need to have a degree in child development or be a professional golf instructor to make use of this guide. It can be easily understood by anyone.

So get ready to gain a lot of insight into how little ones learn this game and how they can become better because of you—not despite you. And who knows, you just might pick up a bit of insight about how you learn the game yourself! I know you'll enjoy the presentation in the following pages by Ireland's best contributor to golf here in the United States, Detty Moore.

Sandra H. Eriksson

Class A Member, LPGA T & CP Division

Director of Golf,
Delray Beach Golf Club, Delray Beach, Florida

LPGA T & CP National Professional of the Year, 1999

Former Winner,
LPGA Sarah Hunter Award for Junior Golf Promotion and Excellence

Introduction

My love for golf did not emerge until I was 24 years of age. I enjoyed playing sports from a very early age. Green fields, sports, and the outdoors are vivid memories from my childhood in Ireland. But opportunities for playing golf were rare in my youth.

We were allowed to play and enjoy sports without constant pushing and interference from adults. Participation was fun, challenging, and exciting. From ages 6 to 12, we organized our own games in the fields or on the street. In high school, we played organized sports: field hockey, netball, baseball, and tennis. But golf was only available to the few kids whose parents were members of a private club, because golf wasn't taught in school.

We could play soccer in a field and have a tennis match on the street, but this was not the case with golf. For golf, you need instruction, special equipment, and—eventually—a golf course. This book can help you give your 6- to 12-year-old children the opportunity I never had. Let me help you introduce your children to golf, a game of a lifetime that can last a lifetime.

So, You're a Baffled Parent!

You may be a parent who knows a lot about golf and plays a good game, but you're not sure how to convey that knowledge to your child. Or you may be an adult who has a basic understanding of golf but little expertise as a player; still, you'd like to introduce a child—yours or someone else's—to this game but you don't know how to go about it. Whatever level of experience you have, if you're reading this book, it's likely you've decided to

Golfers need special equipment, instruction, and, eventually, access to a golf course. But young golfers who get an early start in the game, such as this foursome, develop skills they can use for a lifetime of play.

1

guide a child into the game yourself. Maybe this is a great way to spend more time with your child, or a way to introduce a little person you know to a passion of yours. Maybe there are no junior programs in your area, or you want to ease your child into the game before enrolling her into an organized program. Whatever your reasons, help is at hand in the pages that follow.

This book is designed to help you, the adult, have a successful experience. By "successful" I don't mean you will produce the next Beth Daniel, Karrie Webb, Tiger Woods, or Seve Ballesteros. The advice and drills in this book are designed to help you teach 6- to 12-year-old children the fundamental skills of golf, sportsmanship, teamwork, and—above all else—the fun and rewards of a game they can play for life. Whether you intend to teach your own child or become involved in a group with junior programs as a volunteer, this book will guide you.

How to Use This Book

Teaching Kids Golf: The Baffled Parent's Guide will arm you—whether you're a seasoned player or someone with minimal golfing experience— with the information, skills, drills, and confidence to get a child out on the course and enjoying this wonderful pastime. It's important before we begin to understand that this book will not teach you how to analyze a child's swing or shave strokes from a tournament round. That's a job for a professional. But this book will help you prepare your child to the point where he or she will benefit more quickly from that professional's advice.

Working as a Volunteer

There are numerous junior programs in existence that need volunteers. I run an LPGA Girls Golf Club, and this would be impossible to do without the help of volunteers. It is usually not feasible for fellow professionals to assist on a weekly basis, so assistance from parents or friends is a necessity.

My junior program has 24 kids under age 12. I appreciate any help I receive from parents, but I hand-pick my teachers. Parent volunteers are golfers who have a gentle way with kids and realize that the goal behind the program is to introduce golf in a safe, friendly, and nonthreatening environment. Offer your services as a volunteer, but follow the direction of the professional. For example, you may feel the professional has withheld very important points in his teaching. In your opinion, this is quite possibly an error, so you decide to share those points with the kids. This is wrong. The professional has given the young golfers the basics: your job as a volunteer is to reinforce the basics with tender loving care.

The only qualifications needed to be a great volunteer are

- some knowledge of golf
- a love for children
- patience
- an understanding of the goals of the program

- an ability to make the golf experience fun
- a positive attitude
- enthusiasm
- an ability to call the kids by name
- an ability to be a role model

Teach children at the driving range and on and around the putting green. Build the foundation for their knowledge of the game by incorporating fun games. Practice using gamelike situations to prepare them as quickly as possible to get them on the golf course. Children and adults alike must be educated on the rules of safety and etiquette as well as play fundamentals before taking their game to the course. Some children are prepared for the golf course earlier than others. Children will always have more playing time on and around the green, and they will not be physically capable of playing more than a few modified holes.

Kids don't need a bagful of clubs. You can start them with two or three clubs and a shortened *fairway*, that closely mowed area between the teeing ground and the green. I'll show you how. There are lots of games for kids that can and should be played on and around the green, and even in your backyard, for that matter.

Remember that the golf course is not a kids' playground. Naturally, children should not go out on the course alone unless they are old enough and understand the rules of golf and golf etiquette (see page 11 for guidelines on taking children to a golf course).

As your child's skills improve—and this book will do that—it is important that you have your child's swing evaluated by an LPGA (Ladies Professional Golf Association) or PGA (Professional Golfers' Association) professional at a local facility. Many driving ranges and most golf courses employ certified professionals who would be happy to perform this analysis. Once your child is playing regularly, these periodic check-ups will prove to be helpful. An early correction to a minor flaw will prevent bigger problems from arising later on. But remember for now that we are teaching them to play golf rather than perfecting their swings.

Teaching Kids Golf: The Baffled Parent's Guide is a golf bag full of skills, drills, and tips necessary for taking the swing to the course. It is designed to help you teach children the basics of good golf, including fundamental skills, basic rules, etiquette, and course management. While you should certainly read this book as a whole, it is best to follow the logical format and teach the sound fundamentals.

The earlier chapters in this book will provide you with an understanding of the rich history of the sport, its rules, the equipment you'll need, and the basic elements of swinging a club and putting that little white ball in the hole. Creating a positive atmosphere is perhaps the single most important facet of teaching your kids a game they can enjoy forever, and that is where we start in chapter 1. Chapter 2, Before Hitting the Course: Golf in a Nutshell, and chapter 3, The Journey of a Lifetime, offer explanations on the evolution of golf and golf equipment. Chapter 4 teaches the fundamentals of grip, posture, and alignment for a sound foundation on swinging a club. The skills necessary to take the game to the course are covered in the last four chapters of the book.

Using Skills and Drills

Within each of the skills chapters, you'll find a treasure trove of illustrated drills and games designed to teach the basic skills covered. Once you have a basic understanding of a particular skill—for example, putting or chip shots—you'll find a number of drills and games at the end of the chapter that will give your child a fun way to practice the stroke. These drills are simple and enjoyable, and they're designed to teach kids a necessary skill without making it seem like too much work! To go along with some of these drills, I've developed simple rhymes that kids can recite while practicing. This approach has worked well for me over the years of teaching kids the wonders of the game.

Drills are used for positive reinforcement and to develop swing fundamentals. Through the use of drills, movements may be isolated for improvement. Incorporate these drills for all strokes into your practice sessions.

Remember that no two children take the same approach to learning, and you should modify these drills to suit your child. Not all 6-year-olds are at the same level of maturity or equal in athletic ability or skill level. Because younger children learn differently, I've broken the beginner drills into two segments: for kids from 6 to 8 years, and for kids from 9 to 12 years. Once children have mastered the basics and are ready to move on, you'll find drills for intermediate and advanced play. For quick reference, all drills are labeled with a golf ball symbol to indicate which skill level the drill is appropriate for.

 Beginner 6- to 8-year-old

 Beginner 9- to 12-year-old

 Intermediate to Advanced

This book is written for adults who already have some exposure to golf—whether you are on the course every weekend during your golfing season, or you took some lessons 10 years ago and haven't touched a club since. Although I assume the reader has a basic understanding of the game, I still define special terms. So even if the language of golf is second nature to you, these definitions will remind you that you'll need to explain these terms to a little person who is learning.

At the end of chapters 1, 3, 4, 5, and 6 you will also find useful Question and Answer sections to deal with specific problems. Helpful photos, which you can use as teaching tools, illustrate proper technique. At the end are a glossary, simplified rules, and resources.

Although the principles, drills, and teaching progression in these pages have all worked for me, all teachers have their own style. The common bond good teachers share is a love for the game of golf and the realization that the goal is fun and enjoyment for your son or daughter.

Planning the Lesson

Initially, I recommend exposing your child to golf in an unorganized environment to create an interest in the game. But once your child shows interest, your effort must be organized. You must have your lessons planned, keep the appointments, and encourage politeness and respect.

When you are helping with a technique or skill, it is not a two-way conversation: your wish is his command, and you are the sole authority figure at the lesson. Create an environment that fosters improvement, fun, and respect. Commend your child for his enthusiasm. Establish a routine that reinforces good habits.

At the beginning, keep the sessions short. Most kids just want to hit the ball. That is fine, but your emphasis at the beginning should be on the *short game* (putting and chipping). The skilled and less skilled alike will have immediate success here, and you might spend many hours playing and practicing around the green. If the child is competent in this area, then the transition to the golf course will be smoother.

As your child improves, she will begin to set her own personal standards for improvement. Remember, if she thinks she can do it, she most probably can. Remember also that your child may never progress beyond the basic skills. Your job is to build the solid foundation of grip, posture, and alignment.

Before heading out on the course, make sure children understand basic rules and etiquette. Then let a professional guide them to the next level.

Introduce this wonderful game of golf to your child and then give him space. You can plant the seed, but allow it to bloom in its own time. Your child's motivation will only come from a desire within. Be realistic about what you want for your child. It is important to remember that your child must want to become a better golfer first in order to succeed: it must be the child's dream and not *your* dream. Introduce the game of golf and then allow your child to initiate further sessions.

Allow your child to take many lessons from golf—from the success and disappointments, from the fun and excitement. Golf, just like life, teaches lessons in success and failure. But remember at all times that golf is recreation and your son's success or failure in golf is not a reflection of you, or an indication of his chances for success in life.

The wonderful thing about golf is that your child may practice at the driving range, on the golf course, in a field with modified holes, or even indoors. Your child's first introduction to golf may have been going to the golf course to ride in the cart with you, or going to the driving range while Mom or Dad hit balls, or seeing golf on television. Wherever the seed was planted, please tend to it gently, water it, feed it, and love it—so that it may someday mature into a beautiful person who happens to play golf.

Teaching Kids Golf:
The Baffled Parent's
Guide

CHAPTER 1

Creating a Positive Atmosphere

Before you introduce the tradition of golf to your child, you must answer one question: why do you want your son or daughter to play this wonderful game? If your answer is to produce miniatures of Karrie Webb or Tiger Woods, then this book is not for you. If your answer is to create an atmosphere of fun, enjoyment, and respect—and to help your child enjoy the journey of this learning process—then keep reading.

Few adults are confident they possess unlimited patience when it comes to teaching kids, no matter how much they love them. But it's actually not that hard to teach children if you keep one or two basic principles in mind. Before becoming an LPGA Teaching Professional in 1987, I was very fortunate to have a background in physical education, and I continue

Golf is a difficult game. When you are working with a child on her game, remember that kids universally respond to positive reinforcement and to tasks that are challenging but fun.

to work in education today. My teaching experience over the years in Ireland, Australia, and the United States comes down to this: all children respond to positive reinforcement and thrive on discipline and authority. Keeping this in mind will help you create a positive atmosphere for a young golfer.

A Word on Teaching

Teaching is a gift: a gift box full of love, wrapped in bright ribbons. This gift exudes lots of positive energy that flows from you to your child. You must be full of the wonders of life, just like a child. Your enthusiasm should be contagious. Establish an environment of fun and respect, and don't forget that golf should be fun and relaxing.

Remember that your priorities as a coach and teacher are to introduce the fundamentals but also to let your child have fun. Nurture your child's skill, but let kids *be* kids, both on and off the course. Since hitting a small white ball off a tee or fairway is a difficult task, begin on the putting green by implementing fun games. This will introduce a child to the enjoyment and satisfaction of the game with a minimum of frustration. And remember to gear your instruction to a child's maturity and ability level.

Communication is also key, and how you communicate with a child is important in producing good results. Education professionals often classify children as different kinds of learners. An *auditory* child responds best to clear explanations of a certain task. A *visual* learner will pick up skills best if you demonstrate how they are done or show her a picture. A *kinesthetic* learner picks up skills quickly by getting in there and doing it. Discover how your child learns best, and use appropriate teaching methods.

Be a Role Model

Mom and Dad, you are your child's role model. It isn't, "Do as I say, not as I do." If you are a golfer, you must show respect, tolerance, and patience on the course, just as you do in life. Parents unable to take control of their emotions have no business introducing golf to their children, because children take their lead from adults. If you throw or bang your club, why shouldn't they? If you scream after a bad shot, what does that show them? Respect is a learned skill. By your words and actions, make it known that all players—young and old—must show respect, tolerance, and patience during their practice and play.

Be Encouraging

Golf is a difficult game and can set the least skilled players up for failure. It is your responsibility to encourage, reinforce, and eliminate any sense of failure. Remember that children are like flowers: they bloom at different stages. Promote an atmosphere of being the best you can be. Your children should end each session feeling good about themselves and about their experience.

Your child must learn that while winning and losing is all part of the game, how she deals with both is most important. In the case of golf, an intricate game in which a slight change in grip or posture could result in a bad shot, a player can "win" and "lose" with every swing. A good, rewarding shot can be followed by three bad ones. Keep in mind that in order to win, your child must have sound fundamentals, and this requires hard work and practice.

Competition is healthy. As a coach and teacher, you can incorporate drills that are fun but also expose your child to a competitive environment in a gamelike situation. Eventually, your child will become more skilled and might join local PGA or LPGA youth programs, which sponsor clinics and competitions for junior players. Emphasize that winning is not everything, but what you put into your game is everything. Teach your child to learn from his losses. Teach him to never criticize the opponent and never make excuses. Your child must answer one question: "Did I try until the last ball dropped in the hole?" If the answer is yes, then he is a winner. As you read on into this chapter, you'll find more specific guidelines for helping a child deal with competition and winning and losing.

You can also encourage your children to become involved in other organized team sports. This will help them to be more respectful and tolerant in the game of golf.

Although golf isn't an organized team sport the same way basketball or soccer is, learning about winning, losing, and competition in general is just as important in golf.

Taking the Game to the Course

Kids like to play. Whether it's golf, soccer, or any other activity, they want to get out and start, immediately! Many adults start out on the driving range, but it's important for children to develop skills other than driving before they join you on an actual golf course. The secret to teaching kids golf is to prepare them on backyard minicourses and greens with drills and games that are fun, low pressure, and skills oriented. Once kids can do all of the following, you can consider taking them on a "real" golf course:

- putt and chip
- hit a ball from A to B (along the ground is OK)
- understand and follow the rules of etiquette

In later chapters you'll learn everything you'll need to know to get kids hitting balls properly. After all, that's what it's all about. But before heading into those details, here are secrets for making the most of your child's time on the course.

Pick the Right Times to Play

There are two important timing issues when considering taking a child to the golf course for the first time. The first has to do with the timing in the child's development as a golfer, and the second has to do with the time of day and day of the week you actually show up at the course.

Once the child can do the three basics listed above, find out from the professionals at local courses how "kid-friendly" the courses are. Is there a minimum age for children accompanied by an adult? Are children allowed on the driving range and the practice putting green? Are times set aside each week for kids to play? Can the professional recommend certain days of the week or slow times? The slowest times are best, so be sure to avoid very busy times such as weekend mornings and holidays.

Call the pro shop in advance to reserve a *tee time* (the time at which your group tees off from the first hole). If possible, arrange ahead of time to make a foursome with another adult and child to reduce the likelihood that you and the child will be paired with two adults—the adults probably won't like that much, and it could increase your child's tension about this first expedition. Arrive at the course at least 30 minutes before tee time to sign in, pick up a scorecard, and warm up so you're both prepared to start on time.

Match the Course to Your Child's Skill Level

Adjust the length of each hole to suit your child's skill level. For 6- to 7-year-olds, for example, play 100 yards from the green. Move 150 yards from the green for 8- and 9-year-olds, or move 125 yards in front of the *forward*

There is no such thing as a typical course. Here is a modified 9-hole layout, with pars listed.

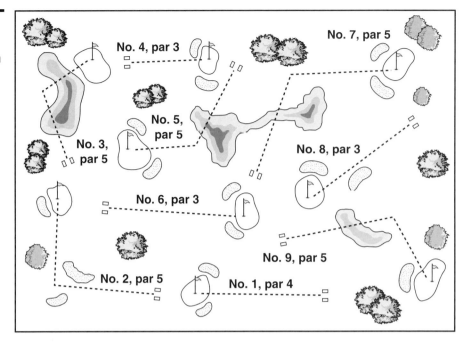

tees (the set of tees closest to the green; most scorecards give yardages for all tee markers). Allow 10- to 12-year olds to play from the forward tees, provided they have the essential skills. Basically, a child's skill level should dictate the distance you play from the green.

On the course, make the goals achievable and keep the playing fun. Playing an *executive course* (a golf course that is slightly shorter than a regu-

For a younger golfer's confidence, have her begin her first drive 100 yards from the hole.

lation course and has mainly par-3 holes), is a wonderful way to introduce your child to the game. Look for this type of course in your area. You can also set up your own course in a large open space, such as an athletic field. Be creative: use hoops, cones, flags, talcum powder, and ropes to set up a teeing ground, a fairway, hazards, and a green. You can even design your own scorecard for the course layout. Initially, use *short-distance golf balls*—also called *Cayman* balls—which are designed to travel only about 50 percent the distance of regular balls.

In addition to modifying the length of the course for your young golfers, you will also need to modify the *par*, the standard of scoring excellence for each hole, to suit your child's age and ability. Read on for tips on introducing young golfers to scoring.

Keeping Score

There is no need to keep score at the beginning. Children enjoy the thrill of hitting the ball, and then going after it to hit it again. Many 6- to 12-year-old children will show more interest in checking out the ducks and turtles rather than playing the game. You will notice about 6- to 8-year-old children that

- they love to hit the ball and run after it
- they skip, run, and are happy
- they observe and ask questions about the nature around them: ducks, turtles, birds, trees, and flowers
- although they understand the rules of safety, they do not necessarily have spatial awareness and do not foresee danger
- for the most part, they are not focused

Be prepared for this! Allow them to smell the roses along the way; in time they will develop the golf bug. Your job is to introduce them to the game.

Children's first experiences with keeping score should take place on the practice putting green, on backyard minicourses, and at the driving range, before they get to an actual golf course. Let children design their own scorecards for the putting green.

You can introduce a child to the format of scoring at the driving range. She can use the targets on the range and visualize playing a golf hole. This will familiarize her with a par 3, 4, or 5 and the clubs she should use to get from tee to green. Instill the same preshot routine for each shot, from the full swing to putts, always approaching from behind the ball (see full explanations in chapter 6).

Although it's not always necessary to keep score, your child should understand how the scorecard works. When you get to the golf course, have

Letting children design their own scorecards gets them thinking about the putting green or minicourse in a practical way and allows "par" to be set at a realistic and nondefeating level.

Putting Green Scorecard

Hole	1	2	3	4	
Par	3	4	5	3	15
Kerry	4	4	4	2	14

Date: June 3, 2001
Scorer: Kerry
Attest: _____

Back Nine 150 YD. Markers IN
Scorecard

Hole	10	11	12	13	14	15	16	17	18	IN
Par	3	4	4	5	3	5	4	4	4	36
Kerry	4	6	5	7	4	4	5	5	6	46
Putts	2	3	2	3	1	2	2	3	2	20

Date: Dec. 3, 2001   Scorer: Kerry
Attest: _____

your child pick up a scorecard. Show her how the scorecard lists the yardage for each hole and the course. There may also be an illustration of the layout of each hole. Point out the space for each player's name, where to record the score for each hole, and the process of adding up the total score for 9 and 18 holes. Show her the space for each player's signature.

Don't put adult standards on your child's shots and actions on the course. For example, I once had five groups of four juniors playing a few

Rating/Slope											
Blue 70.1/122 White 68.6/119 Red 70.9/120											

USGA PACE RATING 4 Hrs.

Hole	1	2	3	4	5	6	7	8	9	Out
Gold	291	175	360	211	387	373	410	520	533	3260
White	278	161	315	200	371	327	383	506	509	3050
Par	4	3	4	3	4	4	4	5	5	36
Handicap	18	10	12	6	2	8	4	14	16	
John	7	4	8	6	7	6	8	10	9	65
Red	267	147	305	139	292	289	342	468	434	2683
Par	4	3	4	3	4	4	4	5	5	36
Handicap	10	16	6	18	14	12	2	4	8	

Date: August 17, 2001   Scorer: John   Attest:

Your 12-year-old's scorecard could look something like this after a season of play.

holes from the 100-yard mark. I spent a little time with each foursome, and in one of the groups, the first boy hit the ball toward the target in the air. My comment was, "Great shot!" The next girl hit her ball a long distance along the ground. I was about to say "Don't worry, you'll hit the next one better," until I heard her say in delight, "Wow, that was the best shot I ever hit!" She skipped after the ball to hit it again (I don't recommend you allow your child to run all over the course, but remember that skipping is a sign of happiness).

The purpose was to hit the ball from the teeing ground to the green, and she had hit the ball a long way—in fact, it went much farther than the boy's lofted ball. She was delighted, but an adult would have been embarrassed with a similar shot, which is why we advise adult beginners to learn the fundamentals on the driving range before going on the course. Allow children to play *golf* rather than play *swing*.

Play the Ball as It Lies

In the beginning, let your child *tee the ball up* (stick a tee in the ground and place the ball on it), for each shot; this will ensure better results. When your child's skills improve, she will want to *play the ball as it lies* (play the ball from the spot where it came to rest). I cannot emphasize how strongly I feel about playing the ball as it lies, which is a rule of golf. I see too many adults and children improving their lies: you must learn to play the ball as it lies if you expect your child to do so in the spirit of the game. In a similar fashion, don't give your child a 2-foot putt for birdie and then boast to everyone that he had his first birdie: he didn't have a birdie unless he putted the ball into the hole.

Keep Them Challenged

Constantly create challenges for young golfers on the course. For example, keep scorecard account only of their putts for the holes played. They can then try to improve their score the next time they play. Or, keep a record of the single putts, or the number of fairways hit, or how many times they hit the ball into the air. This type of minigame within the game helps your child focus without feeling she has to keep official score. This also alleviates the pressure of having to hit the ball a long way. Make scorecards to suit their game and the course.

At this point—as you'll learn in this book—most emphasis should be placed on chipping and putting during course time, so try to get your kids to focus on those skills while playing. Have them use their scorecard to record how positive (P) or negative (N) their attitudes were. Did they get upset at any time? Set a goal of having a scorecard with no Ns.

Limit the strokes for the beginner. If she does not reach the green in a predetermined number of strokes, pick the ball up and place it on the green. Allow a certain number of putts to get the ball in the hole. Allow only one practice swing before each shot. if you allow the kids to *golf*, the game and score will take care of themselves later. Continue to modify the hole until she's ready for the forward tees.

By the time kids are ready to play from the forward tees, they must have a good understanding of golf course etiquette, rules of play, and keeping score.

Competition

Competition in golf should be between your child and the course. Teach him the following characteristics that exemplify the way a good golfer approaches the game.

- play with heart
- give 100 percent to practice and play
- play hard
- have respect for the game
- have respect for the course
- have respect for the opposition
- have a positive attitude at all times
- use a preshot routine
- visualize every shot
- play in the present
- set reachable goals

When your child played a golf hole on the range, he used his imagination to design each hole with rough, hazards, trees, fairway, and green. He then visualized where he would play the shot, down the center or right or left of center. He may do exactly the same on the golf course before he hits each shot.

Play Your Own Game

Every time your child goes on the golf course she has an opportunity to display good sportsmanship and her strengths and weaknesses, both mentally and physically. She will hit good and bad shots and get good and bad bounces in a round of golf. How she deals with these situations will be the difference in the end result. She must concentrate 100 percent for every shot, she must play hard, follow her preshot routine, and play in the present, which is playing one shot at a time. The most important issue for a junior golfer is not to be intimidated by her playing partners. All players have strengths and weaknesses: some are long hitters while others have a terrific short game. Teach your child to always play her own game and to follow the guidelines below.

- be realistic about your golfing ability
- be positive (no complaining or whining); do not waste energy on negative thoughts
- be patient
- follow a preshot routine for every shot
- give 100 percent to each shot
- anchor the good shots
- praise yourself for a good shot by saying "great shot," and don't dwell on the bad shots
- always appreciate the good golf of your playing partner: jealousy is not an option

At the end of the round, your child is a success if she can say, "I did my very best on every shot and that was the best golf and score that I could return today."

Winning and Losing

The definition of growing is learning along the way, and that journey is as important as the end product. Your child will learn from you along that journey, so you can talk a good talk, but you must also walk that talk. Remember that actions speak louder than words. There will always be winners and losers, but how those individuals *respond* to winning and losing is most important.

A good sport must accept the results with a good attitude, so teach

Never Good Enough

I like to relate this story to parents of my junior golfers because it illustrates what not to do when you are teaching a child to golf.

A friend was a ranked junior player who said that the game ceased being fun. No matter how well she played, it was never good enough for her father. After every game, he would criticize her mistakes and replay every shot. Her father had apparently made a big investment in her golf game and expected results. But a child is not a commodity. Don't concentrate on the score; concentrate on the good points. Encourage, praise, and nurture your child along, without pressure. Let her play the game, and then leave it at the golf course. Do not recount every shot when you get home, or, just as it was for my friend, the game will stop being fun and your child may want to quit.

your child to maintain perspective after a win or a loss—and remember, it is not life! Remind your child to put himself in the other guy's shoes, and remind him that "success" is never giving up. Teach your child that success is reaching your potential and having fun along the journey. Keep away from judging success and failure by the score.

If your child can answer "yes" to the following questions, she is a success and you have done a good job.

- are you always honest and fair on the golf course?
- are you having fun?
- are you learning something?
- are you showing respect for yourself, your playing partner, and the golf course?
- are you playing to please yourself and not your parents?

Remember that the most skillful golfer does not always win. The less skillful golfer who grinds through good and bad shots will come out on top in the end.

Misbehaving on the Course

Being an exhibitionist through temper tantrums and club throwing is a reflection of the character of your child. He must learn to control his emotions on the course. By doing that, he can only become a better golfer. If your child misbehaves in practice or play, he must be reprimanded quietly. Do not make a spectacle or embarrass him. Give him guidance and help him find more constructive ways to focus his emotions. If he misbehaves a second time, you must remove him from the course: he will learn from the experience.

Remind him that golf is a privilege and not a right. Of course, he will never learn if you, the parent, cannot control your emotions on the course. Your child will know what is acceptable behavior through your example, both at home and on the golf course.

Teach your kids to play in the spirit of the game and emulate Arnold Palmer, Jack Nicklaus, Kathy Whitworth, and Nancy Lopez. These champions have won and lost with grace and they are wonderful role models.

A Word on Physical Conditioning

Very young children spend a lot of time running about or, hopefully, playing team sports. At the beginning of a golf session young kids don't need a lot of flexibility exercises. Allow them to swing a pitching wedge (which is shorter and slightly heavier than the other clubs) a few times to loosen up. If your child is active in several sports, there is little need for special physical conditioning for golf. Unfortunately many young people spend hours sitting in front of a computer or television screen and get very little physical conditioning. If golf is the only sport your child participates in, then he should follow a conditioning program. He should do some aerobic exercise combined with flexibility exercises three to five times a week and eventually follow a strength-training program when he is older. Being physically fit will enhance your game. Remember that golf is a walking game and juniors are expected to walk in tournaments. My recommendation is that kids and adults who are physically able should always walk. Play golf as it should be played, and incorporate the USGA motto: "a call to feet, golf is a walking game."

Questions and Answers

Q. What is the appropriate age to introduce golf to my child?
A. A child can carry a plastic club when they're still using a high chair. (Legend has it that Tiger Woods watched from his high chair as his father practiced in the garage.) But when it comes to playing, you can introduce playing golf with children's clubs as early as 5 or 6 years of age.

Q. What skills should I begin with?
A. Begin with fun games on the putting green. Then proceed to chipping and eventually move to the full swing.

Q. How often should I work with my child?
A. As often as your child wants to. Your child may want to practice everyday, or he may want to play once or twice a week. She may practice on the putting green daily. Remember, all you are doing is instilling a love for the game.

Q. My child never asks to hit golf balls and only does so if I insist.
A. After you have introduced the game and hopefully instilled a love of

golf by not dictating how and when he plays the game, your child will respond in his own time. Perhaps it is time for you to give him space and allow him to ask Mom or Dad to come and play golf.

Q. My child only wants to go to the course to drive the cart.

A. This is where discipline plays a part. No child under the age of 16 should drive a cart. But as you familiarize her with the game, you can let her ride with you. I recommend that all children walk and play in the tradition of the game. They should take the time to experience and enjoy the beauty and serenity of their surroundings.

Q. My son calls me at work to come home early to hit balls. But when I arrive, he has changed his mind and has become involved in a soccer game with friends.

A. How wonderful to see him involved in team sports! Still, this is the time to learn about respect. He made the arrangement and must keep the appointment. You must explain respect and commitment. Try to use examples and reverse the roles. How would he feel if you went to dinner with business associates after promising to go fishing with him? He will quickly appreciate the importance of respect and commitment. You must demand respect in a positive and consistent manner.

Q. Should I allow my daughter to play on the course without the adequate skills?

A. The answer is absolutely *no*. She should have the basic fundamentals in all areas. Some children will be prepared earlier than their peers; others will be ready later. All children should begin with modified games.

CHAPTER 2

Before Hitting the Golf Course: Golf in a Nutshell

Introduction to Golf

Golf is a complicated game if we let it be. The United States Golf Association (USGA), in conjunction with the Royal and Ancient Golf Club of St. Andrews, publishes the annual *Rules of Golf* as a book well over 100 pages long; the USGA's *Decisions on the Rules of Golf* is 600 pages. Watch a professional event long enough and you'll see a player consulting a blazered official about a difficult situation. And these are golfers who play every day.

I'll explain the most important rules for teaching children in a *simple* and understandable manner. The word *simple* here is important: *golf can be a complicated game because we complicate things*. I intend to keep my teaching simple.

A friend's definition of golf has little to do with the rigidity and rules of golf, however: "The delight of the pure shot; the beauty of the terrain, the wildlife, the flowers, the rivers, the lakes; the peacefulness and how it centers one. The opportunity of meeting new people, how it tests honesty and reveals frailties, and above all the difficulty of the game and the challenge to continue to do your best in somewhat frustrating situations." In a nutshell, golf is a fun, challenging, and difficult game that can be played from an early age. It's a game you can play with your kids, your parents, and even alone.

Getting Started

Golf is becoming increasingly popular, and most professionals realize that children are the future of the game and encourage them to play. But because of that growing popularity, most courses these days are busy with scheduled tee times and foursomes playing one after the other. Again, check with your local professional about the best times or days to bring kids onto the course.

This chapter gives a general overview of the game, the course, and an introduction to sound fundamentals, golf rules, and etiquette. As you're getting started, it's important to keep things as simple as possible. Keep the rules to a minimum:

- Get the ball from the *teeing ground* (the area at the start of each hole, with colored markers identifying varying skill levels) and into the cup using the clubs in your bag—typically a combination of woods, irons, and a putter—in the fewest strokes possible.
- Play the ball where it lies.
- Be honest.
- Be safe. When you hit the ball and it threatens to land near other golfers, call "Fore!" This is a warning cry that tells golfers to turn away from the call and duck their heads.
- Have fun.
- Show respect for yourself, your playing partner, and the golf course.

The most important rule for you as a coach is this: let children play and have fun. Don't worry about too many rules at first. You'll know when the time is right to go into detail about the rules. But remember that in order for you to impart knowledge to your child, you must first have that knowledge yourself. Walk with your child onto the course. Show them the *teeing ground*, from which they hit each hole's first shot. Walk the *fairways* to the *green*, explaining the rules as you go along. After your walk, use a diagram or a chalkboard (or even a marked-up bedsheet) to show all the components of a typical hole, including *teeing ground*, *rough*, *hazards* (bunker and water), *green*, and *out-of-bounds* (see the glossary for definitions). This will reinforce what they've just seen.

In soccer, basketball, and baseball, the fields conform to a worldwide standard. In golf, however, no two golf courses—the playing field for the game—are alike, thanks to design, terrain, weather conditions, and other idiosyncrasies. Even on a single course, from day to day course officials might change features such as the location of the cup on a green or the position of the markers on the teeing ground to ensure more even wear. The one thing all golf courses have in common is that each one has 9 or 18 holes. An 18-hole course is divided into the *front 9 holes* (also known as the *out 9*), which are the first 9 holes, and the *back 9 holes* (the *in 9*), the second set of 9 holes. Each golf hole varies in length.

Using a variety of clubs, each designed for a specific purpose, the golfer makes her way from the teeing ground to the hole on the green. We'll discuss clubs in more detail in chapter 3, but remember for now that you'll have a club called a *driver*, which is designed to hit for distance off the tee; clubs called *irons*, which are used to give you height and distance from the fairway; and clubs such as *pitching wedges* and *sand wedges*, which

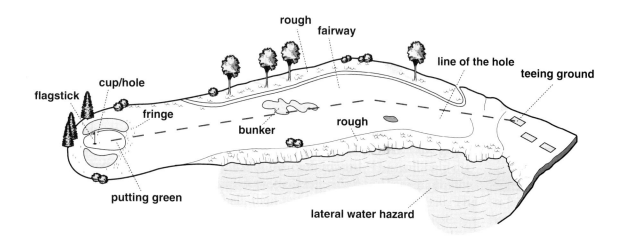

A typical golf hole presents challenges from tee to cup.

are used for special situations. Finally, you'll have a *putter* for the final strokes on the green.

Each hole starts at the teeing ground, continues along the fairway, and ends at the green, the clear area of short grass where the hole (or cup) is situated. You start by hitting the ball off the tee and finish by tapping the ball into the hole on the green. The object of the game is to get the ball into the hole with as few swings (*strokes*) as possible. Count the number of swings you've made at the ball and you're playing golf. It's that simple. Unlike soccer, basketball, and baseball, the player with the lowest number of points, called strokes, wins.

A Typical Scenario on the Course

As a coach, you'll spend some time walking with your child on the course. Since it might have been a while since you played yourself, here's a typical scenario to refresh your memory of the kinds of decisions and situations kids face on just one hole.

You're playing a 125-yard par 3, the shortest hole on the course. Between the tee and the green is a small pond, and the green is neatly sand-wiched between two deep, sandy *bunkers* (hazards covered with sand). You could avoid a direct shot over the pond by hitting off to the side, but you opt instead to take the shortest path to the green and hit directly over the pond. It's a daunting shot. You top your shot off the fairway and the ball skitters to a stop just at the edge of the pond. Your first thought, with a sigh of relief, is that at least your ball didn't go into the water. Your next shot, if you loft the ball properly, is an "easy" 20 yards over the pond to the green, But the gremlins strike again; you hit the ball too hard and too low and it hits the green and skips off the back side. You've now taken three strokes and you're not even on the green yet. You next tap the ball, which sits on the apron of the green, toward the hole. Too hard again. The ball rolls past the cup by 15 feet. You take a deep breath, pull out your putter and cautiously and intentionally take two putts to put the ball in the hole. Six strokes on a par 3. Not bad for a beginner, you say to yourself. Then you move onto the next hole, which is a long par 5 with a dogleg and thick ball-eating woods on either side of the fairway.

In addition to the smoother and closely mowed grass of the fairway, the typical hole may also have *rough*, which is longer, thicker grass on each side of the fairway; *hazards*, which are sand bunkers or water; and *out-of-bounds* areas, where play is prohibited. If you hit a ball into the out-of-bounds area, you'll be penalized. The rough should naturally be avoided for a number of reasons. First, the longer grass makes it difficult to take a smooth swing and connect cleanly with the ball; second, because the rough is off to the side, it's more difficult to land the ball on the green or in the fairway from there. Hazards are located at strategic places on the course. You will find bunkers bordering the fairway, known as *fairway bunkers*, or around the green, called *greenside bunkers*.

Water hazards are classed into two categories. *Regular hazards* cross the fairway and are marked with yellow stakes or lines. *Lateral hazards* run parallel to the fairway and are marked with red stakes or lines.

Balls in the longer grass of the *rough* present a challenge—both to hit and to find.

The beauty and layout of the playing area changes with every shot. As a coach and parent walking alongside your child on a beautiful golf hole, it's easy to help her appreciate the wonders of nature and the game of golf.

The teeing ground is the rectangular area identified by colored markers (colors vary by course). The teeing ground extends two club lengths back from the markers. You can tee your ball up between the markers or within two club lengths behind the markers. Never tee up in front of the markers. There are usually at least three sets of markers. The forward set closest to the hole

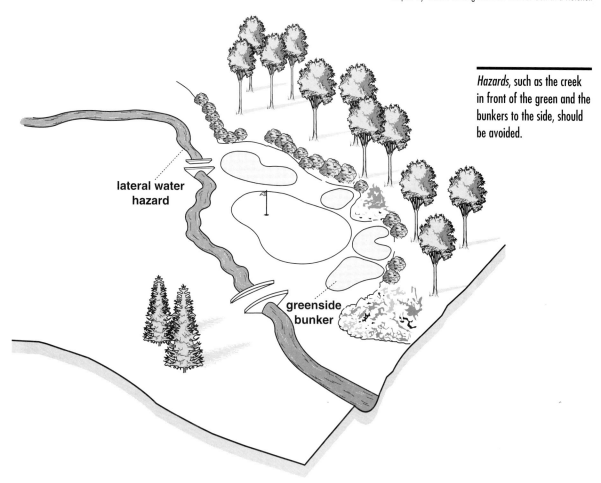

lateral water hazard

greenside bunker

Hazards, such as the creek in front of the green and the bunkers to the side, should be avoided.

identifies the *forward teeing ground*; the next set, which is the second-closest set to the hole, is the *regular teeing ground*; the *championship* (or *back*) teeing ground is the third set, which is farthest from the hole. By playing from the championship tee markers you lengthen the course, thus making it

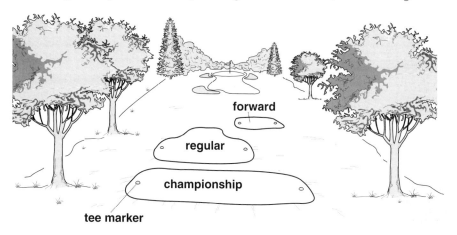

forward

regular

championship

tee marker

Golfers choose which *teeing ground* to launch their first shots from.

more difficult. The forward teeing ground is suitable for juniors, women, beginners, and seniors.

When you are starting kids out, it's best to modify the game for them. Instead of hitting from a distant tee, have them tee off 100 yards from the green, in the center of the fairway. This is the area where you'd hope to land your ball. The putting green, whose closely cropped grass is not unlike a pool table, is beautifully manicured so a ball can roll smoothly. But the green, unlike a pool table, is not flat. It can roll, slant, or undulate, and each twist adds a putting challenge. A good golfer will learn to read the green and make putts that take advantage of the green's topography. The cup or hole on the green is identified by a flagstick at least 7 feet in height.

Scoring

The standard of scoring excellence, the number of strokes per hole, is called *par*. The par is expressed as a par 3, par 4, or par 5—depending on the length of the hole. A par 3, a shorter hole requiring fewer strokes, is the shortest hole; a par 5 is the longest. All distances are measured in yards. A par 3 on a regular course is as long as 250 yards; a par 4 is 251 to 470 yards; a par 5 is anything above 471 yards.

You don't want a child's first foray onto the course to begin with a 400-yard par 4. Instead, shorten the course to make it accessible to his skills and have him hit his first shot off the fairway from 100 yards out. In fact, courses are adjusted and shortened substantially in junior competitions.

The length of the hole dictates how many shots it should take to get the ball on the green, and that number of shots is known as getting on the green *in regulation*. A par 3 is designed for a golfer to reach the green in one shot from the tee and put the ball into the hole with two putts. A par 4 is designed for two shots to the green and two putts. A par 5 is designed for three shots to the green and two putts. If you put the ball in the cup one stroke below par, you've made a *birdie*; if you put the ball in the cup two strokes under par, you've made an *eagle*. For example, one stroke above par is called a *bogey*; two strokes above par is a *double bogey*.

Be realistic about your child's goals. He will not be able to reach the green in the regulation number of strokes for a very long time. Again, modify the holes according to his strength and skill level. His success will only come from his own interest, knowledge of the skills, practice, and patience.

Basic Rules

The United States Golf Association and the Royal and Ancient Golf Club of St. Andrews together dictate and interpret the rules of golf. The basic rules are simple: play the ball as it lies and leave the course as you found it.

Knowing the rules may help you save strokes and allow you to penalize yourself when appropriate.

In basketball, soccer, volleyball, hockey, and rugby, you have a referee. In golf, players are their own referee. Players must call penalties on themselves—a huge responsibility for a 6- to 12-year-old child. There are 34 basic rules. It's a good idea to invest in an official rules book so you can help your child learn the rules; a good, first rule book for children is the USGA's *Snoopy and Friends*. Focusing on just one or two rules a day, introduce the rules in game situations on the putting green or driving range.

The following sections include the most common situations and penalties incurred in golf. A handy summary of key rules, The Rules Simplified, can also be found in the appendix (see pages 107–8).

No Penalty

In the following situations, a player may obtain *relief,* options for moving the ball without incurring a penalty. She may lift, clean, and drop the ball no more than one club length from where the ball lay to the nearest *point of relief.* She drops the ball by standing erect, holding the ball at shoulder height and at arm's length, and then dropping the ball.

The following are situations where relief can be obtained without penalty.

- ball on a *cart path*
- ball in *casual water*
- ball in ground that is under repair
- ball on the wrong putting green
- ball lying against a sprinkler
- ball embedded in its own *pitch mark*
- ball lying against a staked tree

This player can obtain *relief* from the cart path with a drop and not be penalized.

One-Stroke Penalties

A one-stroke penalty must be added to the score in the following situations.

- Add a penalty stroke when a ball in play is moved at *address*, which is when the player takes her stance and *grounds her club* (places the club on the ground directly behind the ball). The ball must then be replaced to the original position. There is no penalty if the ball moves at address on the teeing ground, since the ball on the tee is not yet considered to be in play.

The out-of-bounds area should be avoided as play is prohibited there. The player who has a lost ball is penalized one stroke plus distance.

- Add a penalty stroke when the ball is lost or hit *out-of-bounds*. The player must play the next stroke from where the original ball was played. You are allowed five minutes to look for a lost ball.

- An *unplayable lie* is when the ball is in such a position that the player is unable to swing, or in such a position that swinging might cause an injury. An example of such a situation is when the ball is up against a tree. The player is entitled to three options for relief under the penalty of one stroke.

  1. She may drop the ball in a spot that is within two club lengths, as long as that spot is not closer to the hole.

  2. She may return to the spot she played her last stroke from.

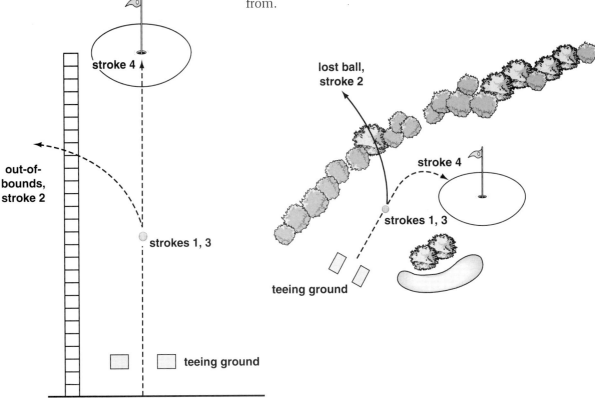

3. She may go back and drop the ball as far back as she wishes, provided she keeps the spot where the ball landed and was rendered unplayable between herself and the hole. If the ball is unplayable in a bunker, she must drop the ball in the bunker.

- A one-stroke penalty can also be added when a ball lands in a *water hazard*. A regular water hazard is a body of water between the player and the hole; it is marked with yellow stakes or lines. The player is allowed three options of relief.

  1. He may play the ball as it lies without incurring a penalty.
  2. He may drop the ball behind the hazard—keeping the point where the ball entered the hazard between himself and the flag—and add a penalty stroke.
  3. He may go back to where the original ball was hit and add a penalty stroke.

- A *lateral hazard* (see art on following page) is a body of water that runs parallel to the fairway and is marked with red stakes or lines. There are five options from here. The three options available from a water hazard (above) apply here. The player may also drop on either side of the hazard within two club lengths and not nearer the hole and add a one-stroke penalty.

The tree presents an *unplayable lie* for this player.

Options for play from a *water hazard.* 1. Play the ball as it lies with no penalty. 2. Go back to the original spot and play another ball (one-stroke penalty). 3. Go back as far as you wish on a line keeping the point of entry into the hazard between you and the flag (one-stroke penalty).

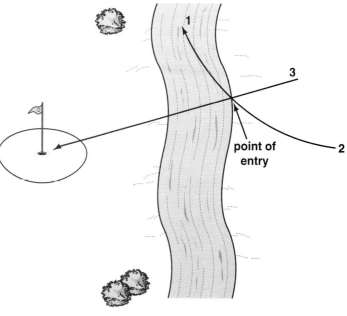

Options for play from a *lateral hazard*. 1. Play the ball as it lies with no penalty. 2. Go back to the original spot and play another ball (one-stroke penalty). 3. Drop a ball within two club lengths of the point of entry (not nearer the hole; one-stroke penalty). 4. Drop a ball within two club lengths on the opposite side of the haz- ard from the point of entry (not nearer the hole; one- stroke penalty). 5. Go back as far as you wish on a line keeping the point of entry into the hazard between you and the flag (one-stroke penalty).

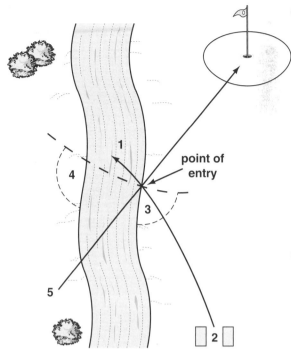

point of entry

- A *whiff*, when the player swings with the intention of striking the ball and misses it, is cause for a one-stroke penalty.

Two-Stroke Penalties

A player is required to take a two-stroke penalty in the following situa- tions.

- If your ball strikes another ball while on the putting green, add two strokes to your score. Play your ball as it lies and replace your playing partner's ball to the original position. It is best to always have an opponent place a coin, which is called a *marker*, behind his ball on the green. He may then lift his ball.

- If your ball strikes the flag while putting on the putting green, you incur a two-stroke penalty. Always ask someone to tend the flag and remove it when necessary. If it is removed, place it away from the line of the putt.

- If you play the wrong ball, you incur a two-stroke penalty. Go back to the spot where your original ball is, play on with the original ball, and only count the strokes played with the original ball and add a penalty of two strokes. If the error is not detected until after you hit from the next teeing ground, you will be disqualified. In *match play* (a type of play where each hole is a separate contest and the player or team who wins the most holes wins), if a player plays the wrong ball, he automatically loses that hole.

- Playing the ball from outside the teeing ground will earn you a two- stroke penalty. You must replay from the correct teeing ground and add the penalty. In match play, your opponent has the option to recall the shot—he may ask you to play the shot again.

- Improving the lie of the ball earns you two strokes. You may not move the ball to a better position or stand behind the ball to flatten the grass.

Always have a playing partner or caddy *tend the flag* while you're putting.

- A two-stroke penalty will result if, in a hazard, you *ground the club* (place the *sole* or bottom of the club on the ground at address or during the back swing). Hold the head of the club off the ground.

Disqualification

The following actions will earn you a disqualification.

- Practicing on the competition course on the day of a *stroke play* competition.
- Playing the wrong ball and not rectifying it according to the rules.
- Playing from the incorrect teeing ground and not rectifying it according to the rules.
- Failing to sign your scorecard.
- Signing a scorecard that is incomplete or incorrect.

Etiquette

Everyone knows that etiquette is acting properly, whether you are talking about how you act at home or on the golf course. Golf's unwritten rules of etiquette are as important as the legal rules of golf, even though you can't incur penalty strokes for poor etiquette.

- Respect your playing partner and the golf course.
- Leave the golf course as beautiful as you found it.
- Pick up trash.
- Act like a lady or gentleman on the course; do not shout or run.

Left: A trip to the bunker can leave a mess. Always rake the sand smooth before you leave.

Right: Replacing your *divots* before moving on is part of good golf etiquette.

- Rake bunkers after you leave them.
- Replace divots.
- Repair ball marks on the green.
- Place bags or carts away from the green, on the side closest to the next teeing ground.
- Do not take practice swings on the teeing ground, for fear of taking a divot.
- Always stand in a position where you will not distract other players.
- Stand facing to the side of other players, never behind them.
- Never move ahead until everyone has hit.
- While on the putting green, do not walk directly on the line of anyone's putt to the hole. Walk around behind the player, or behind the hole.
- Never stand directly behind the cup on the path of the ball.
- Always remove the ball from the cup with your hand, not a club.
- The person with the lowest score on a hole has the *honor* (the right to tee off first) on the next hole.
- The player whose ball is farthest from the hole hits first; that is called *away*.
- The player whose ball is closest to the hole will tend the flag.
- The player who *holes out* (makes it into the cup) first will take the flag and will then be ready to replace it when everyone else has holed out.
- Remain on the green until everyone has holed out.
- Mark the scorecard at the next teeing ground.

- Slow play should be avoided. Keep up with the group in front. If they get more than a hole ahead, allow the group behind you to *play through*.
- Take no more than 13 minutes for each hole.
- Call a loud "Fore!" when you accidentally hit the ball in the direction of someone else.
- When you hear "Fore!", duck your head and turn your back to the direction of the call.
- Only swing the club when everyone else is a safe distance away.
- If you see or hear any signs of lightning, leave the course immediately. Never take shelter under trees. Leave your golf clubs on the course.

If a situation arises and you are unsure of the rules, adapt the courtesies you use in life to your golf game. Do what is fair and honest.

CHAPTER 3

The Journey of a Lifetime

Golf is a journey of a lifetime that you can share with your children. Golfers can begin to play the game when they are as young as 5 or 6 years old, and they can get out on the course and enjoy the game at 80. When you expose your child to golf, you may be bringing him into an activity that will bring lifelong enjoyment and challenge.

This chapter covers the first steps you'll take on this journey together. You'll learn about the history of the game, for the tradition of golf is an important part of the game. Proper-fitting equipment is key to a young golfer's success, and you'll learn how to find the right gear for your child.

History of Golf

Children have great imaginations, and most are intrigued by tales of old. You can use a child's natural love for stories to tell her about the beginnings of the game and to give her an appreciation for the tradition of golf.

The first round of golf ever played is not recorded in the history books, and we don't know who played that first round or where it was played. But the late golf writer and historian Peter Dobereiner has traced golf back to 1296, to the village of Loenen in the Netherlands. There is evidence of golf in Roman times in what is now France, Belgium, and the Netherlands. In 1457, King James II banned golf in Scotland, claiming it was distracting from the practice of archery, which was needed for the defense of the country. In fact, golf was declared unlawful in Scotland on numerous occasions.

The first golf clubs were made of hazel wood and later of ash. Called *featheries*, golf balls were stuffed with feathers and covered with leather. It was not unusual to see women on the course, wearing long skirts; men played in kilts.

The Scots may not have invented golf, but they are responsible for its development. The game as it's played today dates back to Scotland in 1744.

Ten years later, in 1754, the Royal and Ancient Golf Club of St. Andrews in Scotland drafted the basic rules of golf. In 1888, golf was introduced in the United States, in Yonkers, New York. The United States Golf Association (USGA) was established in 1894.

Kids—and here I mean young goats—played a role in early golf. The links courses, which when viewed from above would have been identifiable as designed by nature rather than by architects, were originally inhabited by goats and sheep. The course was built on sandy soil by the seashore, and the natural landscape was scattered with sand dunes, heather, and gorse, but no trees. In 18th- and 19th-century Scotland and Ireland, goats and sheep grazed on the land, thereby eliminating the need for maintenance and equipment.

Kids today—and now I mean children—continue to play a part in the history of golf, in both amateur and professional fields. Teenage twins Aree and Naree Wongluekiet are taking women's golf by storm. Sergio Garcia, the young Spaniard, and of course Tiger Woods are household names to golfers and nongolfers alike.

Clubs

In most other sports, equipment must be fitted to the child. In basketball, the ball is smaller and the baskets are lower; in baseball, the bats are lighter; in tennis, the racquets are smaller and lighter. Golf equipment is no different. Spurred by the interest created by Tiger Woods, many manufacturers are now making clubs for kids as young as 3 years old.

But, there's no way around it: clubs are expensive. And the variety of clubs and accessories to choose from can be confusing. However, properly fitted clubs are vital to the immediate success of a young child's game, so this is an area where you'll need to educate yourself.

Purchasing clubs manufactured for children is a far better alternative than cutting down adult clubs (adult clubs, even when cut down, are too heavy for children and can cause injury and swing faults). Consider buying used clubs if you can find them. There's no point in investing in a new set of clubs your child will outgrow in a season.

When purchasing equipment, seek advice from your local PGA or LPGA professional. He or she will be able to advise you on the best clubs for your child and help you find clubs that meet your cost requirements. But while it's important to seek the advice of a professional for this step, it's important that you understand how the various facets of club choice can affect a swing and your child's progress.

Clubs must be fitted to each child. The club that is suitable for a 6-year-old won't be suitable for a 10- or 12-year-old, and perhaps not even for *another* 6-year-old child. Some companies supply golf equipment made specifically for children, and a local professional who works with kids is probably your best bet for advice.

A properly fitted club is determined by a number of factors, including the child's height, length of arms, and posture. Kids need light, flexible clubs with a properly sized grip. The length of the club will affect how a child will stand to the ball and, ultimately, what kind of contact she'll make with the ball during the swing. If the club is too long, the child will have to grip a few inches farther down the shaft. If the club is too heavy, the child will have a difficult time swinging; this may set the child up for bad swing habits in the future.

How the club sits on the ground is also relevant. This is known as the *lie* of the club. The *sole* of the club should be flat on the ground when a child addresses the ball.

The *grip* of a club is designed to provide the best possible connection between the golfer and the club. The material in the grip—whether leather, rubber, or a synthetic is used— provides a tacky base that's easy to hold. The grip must be child-sized so she can hold the club. A grip that is too small or too large will create tension and affect *ball flight*, which is the trajectory and direction the ball travels.

Take a look at the child's hands on the club. The middle fingers of

Anatomy of a golf club. Pictured here are an iron and a wood.

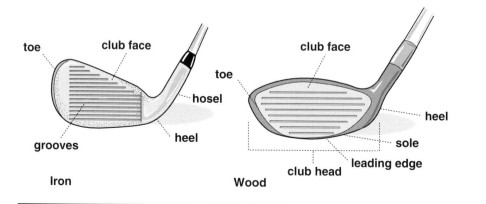

A Word on Distance

The distance a player hits each club is totally dependent on his or her ability and club head speed. The distance and trajectory will also vary according to the club used and its shaft length and face loft.

For example, let's look at an adult's theoretical swing with the same club head speed. The distance between each iron is approximately 10 yards. So a 3-iron will produce a shot that is 10 yards longer than a 4-iron. The same theoretical adult swing produced using a wood would have a slightly longer distance (approximately 10 to 15 yards, with the driver producing the longest shot). With children the distance between each club would be much less.

When you are coaching your child, emphasize that accuracy is far more important than distance. Children will see very little difference in yardage.

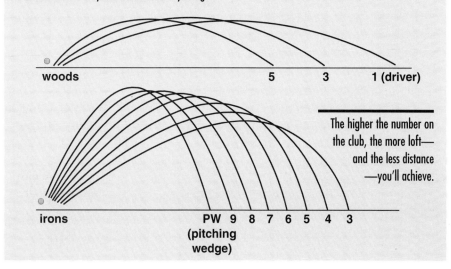

woods   5   3   1 (driver)

The higher the number on the club, the more loft—and the less distance—you'll achieve.

irons   PW 9 8 7 6 5 4 3
(pitching wedge)

Everything But the Clubs

Balls

There are golf balls to suit everyone's game and price range. The most durable ball has a Surlyn cover and is best suited to a beginner. Balata balls are the usual choice for advanced golfers and professionals. A Surlyn-covered ball has a harder feel than the balata; the balata has a softer cover and tends to cut more easily.

Every golf ball is stamped with an identifying number and the manufacturer's name, which helps the player recognize her ball on the golf course. For example, you're playing with a "4" and your partner is using a "3"; this allows you to identify your ball and makes sure you don't inadvertently play your partner's ball during the course of your match. If you're both playing the same brand and number, you can put an identifying mark on the ball with a permanent marker or pencil: maybe a black dot, a flower, or two dots. In fact, all golfers should put a personal identification mark on their balls.

Balls come in different colors, but the traditional color is white. The dimple formation on each ball assists ball flight and trajectory. Due to present-day technology, dimple formation and design change frequently.

There is no need to buy expensive balls for kids. Cheaper balls, even used balls, are quite appropriate for children and for your budget. For children playing in closer quarters—perhaps in a neighborhood field—*short-distance balls* or *Cayman balls*, which travel half the distance of a regular golf ball, make play safer on a short course set up in an open space. And for kids practicing in the backyard, you can purchase *golf whiffle balls*. Soft sponge balls can also be used. About the size of but lighter than a tennis ball, these balls are easier to hit with a light child's club. They come in a variety of bright colors, which appeals to young folk. Beach balls are a good alternative for indoors (gym or garage).

Tees

Tees elevate the ball for your first drive of each hole. They are prohibited on the fairway.

Tees are manufactured from wood or plastic, and they come in different lengths. The tee is used on the teeing ground to put the ball into play. Let the child stick the tee in the ground and put the ball on it; teach him to tee the ball a little higher when using a wood and low when using an iron (or, use a short tee with irons). If the child is interested in the mechanics, here's the explanation: When the ball is on the tee, half of the ball should be above the top edge of the club. Since the face of a wood is deeper than the face of an iron, you need to tee a little higher with the wood to change its position relative to the top of the club.

Shoes

Golf is a walking game, so comfortable shoes are important—don't forget that children take more strides than adults do to cover the same ground. It's possible to spend as much as $200 for a pair of good shoes, but needless to say, considerably cheaper shoes are adequate for most golfers, particularly golfers whose shoe size changes every year. Sneakers are fine for beginning golfers, though once your child has been on a few outings and is developing enthusiasm for golf, purchasing golf shoes with soft spikes will provide him with firmer foot control. Most courses require soft spikes only in golf shoes; sneakers are usually allowed for juniors, but check in advance with the professional. Water resistance is a handy feature in a golf shoe. Golfers should wear thick, comfortable socks with whatever shoe they're wearing; select shoe size to fit.

Bags

Since your child will be playing with a limited set of clubs, the child's first bag should be a lightweight one. Bags come in a variety of colors, weights, and sizes. Purchase one with a stand attached if possible: this will make it much easier to get to the clubs. Children grow out of their clubs and bags quickly, so it's imprudent to sink a lot of money into a golf bag—good-fitting clubs are a better investment.

Manufacturers produce bags for kids as young as 3 years old. These bags only hold two or three clubs and a few balls, which is just right because more clubs would be too heavy for a very young child— allow kids to carry more than two or three clubs, and they're likely to wind up in your bag. Check the classified ads or with a local pro if you'd like to buy a used bag.

A child's first golf bag should be light and easy to carry. A stand is also a nice feature.

Glove

A golf glove is not a necessity. But a glove could improve the child's grip on the club, especially when hot weather produces sweaty palms. A right-hander would wear the glove on the left hand; the left-hander wears the glove on the right hand.

I don't recommend a glove for kids, but if they're going to have one, make sure it fits: a glove that's too big could cause blisters.

The glove is always worn on the target hand for grip, since the club is held in the palm and fingers of the left/target hand.

Clothing

Golf is a game with a long tradition. Golf clothes must be comfortable, but jeans, sweats, and T-shirts are not appropriate attire for the golf course, even for children. Most golf clubs require players to wear a shirt with a collar and dress pants or dress shorts—a polo shirt and khakis or chinos are always acceptable. T-shirts and casual shorts are OK at the driving range, or when your kids are practicing in a field and not at a golf facility. Set the standard early, and your child will respect the golf tradition.

Optional Equipment

Pull carts for golf bags are available, and a cart for your golf bag should be light and well balanced. Kids' pull carts are available, but why not have your child carry his own clubs? After all, juniors are required to carry their bags at tournaments.

Golfers should always be prepared for rain and for cold conditions, so a wind shirt or waterproof suit is ideal for cold and inclement weather. A golf umbrella is optional. A small towel with a loop so it can be clipped to the bag is recommended, so children can clean their balls and clubs.

Questions and Answers

Q. Should I explain the history of golf to my young golfing buddy?

A. All golfers should understand the wonderful tradition of the game. An understanding of some of golf's colorful history can help kids get more involved in the sport—but beware of turning the information into a history lesson!

Q. How do I know if the clubs are too short for my daughter?

A. Check her setup and posture (see page 43, Teaching Grip, Posture, and Alignment). She may have to bend over too much, or she may continually miss the ball. A longer club may be necessary; check with your local professional.

Q. How important is the fit of golf clubs for children?

A. Children need bicycles and skis that fit. Golf clubs need to fit in the same way, and a proper fit is vital. For example, a club that is too heavy will make it difficult for your child to swing. Also, if a club is too long or too short, it will cause your child to compensate. This will be a very difficult habit to correct later.

Q. My son always wants the most expensive clubs. Should I buy them?

A. Proper fitting equipment should be your priority, not price or designer/pro brand names. Remember that kids outgrow equipment quickly. If your child wants a top-of-the-line club, let him buy one with his own money.

Q. I have no idea how to determine what club length is appropriate for my child. How do I figure this out?

A. Here's what to generally look for in a club for a child. A 7-iron suitable for most 3- to 5-year-olds is approximately 23½ inches long. An appropriate 7-iron length for a 6- to 8-year-old is about 28½ inches. For a 9- to 12-year-old, a good length is about 33 inches. My advice is to confer with your local pro.

CHAPTER 4

Fundamentals

Professionals and very good amateur golfers make the game look easy. Long, straight drives rocket down the center of the fairway. Elegant approach shots drop the ball inches from the hole. And calm, reassured putts drop the ball into the cup.

The beautiful, technically sound swings of the better players come from hours of practicing golf fundamentals, and even the most accomplished professionals work constantly to perfect their swings. You know from your own experience that golf is a difficult game. You can't execute consistent golf swings like those of Beth Daniel, Karrie Webb, or Darren Clarke without faithfully practicing the basic fundamentals of grip, posture, and alignment.

These three basic elements of grip, posture, and alignment are the foundation of good golf and the essentials on which everything else is built. These fundamentals must be established before you can teach the essential skills of putting, chipping, pitching, and the full swing, which are covered in upcoming chapters.

Your job is to help your child understand the importance of these fundamentals. Remind him that the best players in the world work hard and continue to focus on the basics. They know these basics are key, for most players will tell you the reason that their swing is out of position is because of bad posture.

These players continually check their *GPA*—grip, posture, and alignment—for better results. By improving her GPA, a child will learn to put her body in a good athletic position that will allow her to swing the club correctly.

Teaching GPA: Grip, Posture, and Alignment

When you first start working with your child, I think it's important initially to use the terms *right* and *left* to avoid confusing children early on with unnecessary terminology. But if I'm working with a group of children who

Target versus Nontarget

Once children have the basics down, spend extra time making sure they understand which is their target side and which is their nontarget side. Use reminders at the beginning of each lesson or practice to reinforce children's familiarity with the terms. That will ensure that children understand your references to target and nontarget sides in instructions. Avoiding using the words *left* and *right* in instructions is especially important if you and the children don't all have the same dominant hand. When you discuss ball flight, remember to reverse the direction for a left-hander (instead of left to right, right to left).

are comfortable with the basics, I begin using *target* to mean "the side toward the hole or target" and *rear* to mean "the side away from the hole or target." These terms make instructions clear for both right-handed and left-handed golfers in group situations. Again, for right-handers, the target side is the left side. For left-handers, the target side is the right side. As we progress through the book, I'll use target and rear designations also so you can easily adapt instructions for both right- and left-handers.

Because grip, posture, and alignment are so important, a mnemonic can help kids repeat and remember these essentials. Make a game of making one up for GPA, or jumble it to spell GAP, a clothing store they might know. Whatever route you go, make it fun.

Here are five keys to effective teaching that you should keep in mind when working with young golfers.

- keep directions simple
- demonstrate skills and techniques correctly
- use photographs as a visual aid (the photographs in this book will work well, and you may also find other good shots of golfers at work)
- allow children to try skills themselves
- ask questions that require kids to think about what they're doing—and give them time to answer!

Remember that kids are eager to get in there and try things. Don't bore or burden them with lengthy explanations: keep the demonstrations and directions short and simple. There are also lots of drills in this book that you can use as activities (see chapters 5 through 8). Now let's look at the most important aspects of any golf swing.

Grip

The correct grip makes it possible to *square the club* at impact, which means the club face is aiming directly at the target rather than right or left of it. The only contact the player has with the ball is through her grip on the club. Her grip affects the position of the club face, and if the grip is correct, the club face will be square and the ball will go straight. An incorrect

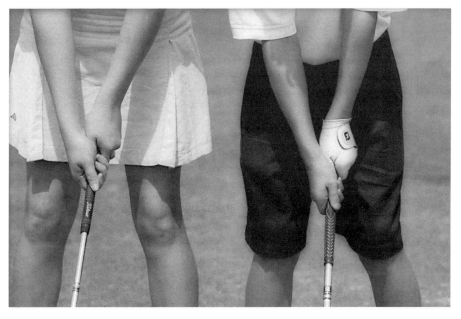

A good grip is an essential component of a good shot.

grip leads to shots that head off to the right or left of the target.

I recommend the *10-finger full-swing grip* for all beginning young golfers and for the small hands of young children. It's also called the *baseball grip*, for in many ways it's like the grip we use to hold a baseball bat. As children grow, they can make the transition to an *interlock grip* or *overlap grip*, though kids with very small hands might need to stay with the 10-finger grip. The illustrations below show you these different grips.

I've mapped out simple, step-by-step instructions for explaining the grip to a right-hander. The designations for target and rear hands are included, so you can easily adapt these for a left-hander.

Younger kids starting out should use the *10-finger full-swing grip* (left), which is simple and comfortable for beginners. The *interlock grip* (center) and the *overlap grip* (right) might prove useful as a young golfer's experience grows.

Your child should stand tall with both hands hanging by his side, thumbs pointing inward. Place the left/target hand on the club by literally shaking hands with the club. The club's grip should run diagonally across the hand in the palm and fingers. He should close his hand around the grip. Grip pressure should be felt in the last three fingers of the left/target hand. The left/target thumb should rest on the inside of the shaft. The thumb and index finger form a V that points between his chin and right/rear shoulder. The grip of the club should rest beneath the heel pad of the left/target hand.

When the left/target hand is in the correct position, he should see two to three knuckles of the left/target hand. Allow him to hold the club out in front of him and place the right/rear hand on the club, just as though he were shaking hands with the club. The club should be gripped in the fingers of the right/rear hand, the right/rear thumb should rest on the left or target side of the shaft. The lifeline of the right/rear hand should fit snugly over the left/target thumb. The index finger and thumb of both hands should form a V that points between the chin and the right/rear shoulder.

The 10-Finger Grip Simplified

Some children may do better with a simplified version of these instructions. Here's a simplified way to teach the 10-finger full-swing grip. These are for a right-hander, but target and rear distinctions are given so you can easily reverse these for a left-hander.

The club must be placed in the hands naturally. Ask your child to show their left/target hand and then their right/rear hand. Use the left/target hand to shake hands with the club. Hold the club on the left/target side of the body, so they can see two to three knuckles of the left/target hand. Now hold the club out in front, extend the right/rear hand, and shake hands with the club.

Teaching the 10-finger full-swing grip.
Left: With the club held in the left/target hand, your golfer should be able to see two or three knuckles.
Center: When placing the right/rear hand on the club, the thumb should rest on the target side of the shaft. The lifeline of the right/rear hand should fit snugly over the left/target thumb.
Right: The index finger and thumb, on both hands, should form a V that points between the chin and the right/rear shoulder.

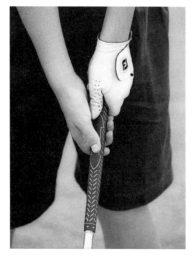

The child should be able to answer three questions. Can she see two to three knuckles on the left/target hand? Is the club gripped in the fingers of the right/rear hand? Are the two Vs formed between the index fingers and thumbs of both hands pointing between her chin and right/rear shoulder? If the answers to all three questions are yes, she's gripping the club correctly. Remind your child to use a light grip pressure.

Posture

In order to swing a golf club you must be in a good athletic position, which is not unlike the ready position in tennis, baseball, or basketball. *Addressing the ball* involves the golfer, with club in hand, assuming a specific preparatory posture and position of feet, knees, hips, shoulders, and body. Check your own address in a mirror so you know *your* posture is correct before you teach your child.

Young athletes demonstrate good athletic posture and position, which are as essential in golf as in other sports.

To address the ball properly, stand tall with feet shoulder-width apart. Bend at the hips with the back straight, knees flexed slightly, and weight evenly distributed on the balls of the feet. Tilt your upper body slightly to the right/rear side (reverse for a left-hander). The ball should be centered in your stance. Keep in mind that as the club's shaft gets longer (lower club numbers), the ball will be placed farther forward in your stance (closer to the left/target side).

The photographs on page 48 illustrate a young golfer's proper address.

Teaching a young golfer to address the ball. 1. Stand tall with the club directly in front. 2. Step forward with the right/rear foot, bend over, and place the club head on the ground. 3. Step forward with the left/target foot to complete the address. 4. A down-the-line view of the proper address.

Have your child follow these three simple steps.

1. Stand tall with the club directly out in front of you (photo 1).

2. Step forward with the right/rear foot. Bend over and place the club head on the ground (photo 2).

3. Step forward with the left/target foot to be fully in the address position (photo 3; photo 4 shows a down-the-line view of the address).

Alignment

Alignment is the placement of the club to the ball and the position of the body—specifically, the feet, knees, hips, and shoulders—in relation to the target. Proper alignment is crucial: if your alignment is incorrect, your shot will be off target. Remember that most shots are played off a *square stance* (that is, square or parallel to the target line).

To keep this simple, tell your child to imagine that she is hitting a ball down a railroad track. The ball is on the outer track, and this outer track runs straight to the target. Her feet, knees, hips, and shoulders are on the inside track, which is parallel to the *target line*—the direct path from the ball to the target.

To gain consistency, your child should practice grip, posture, and alignment daily. Use a mirror as a teaching tool: it will give your child a lot of feedback. She should stand facing the mirror to check her grip and posture. Turning sideways to the mirror, she can check her alignment. (See also Mirror Drills, pages 83–84.)

A Word on Foot Position

Certain circumstances demand that a golfer adjust the position of the feet in setup. Throughout the book you'll find the stance—the position of the feet in relation to the target line in the setup—described as *square*, *open*, or *closed*. In a square stance, both feet are parallel to the target line. In an open stance, the target/left foot is drawn back from the target line and both feet are aimed slightly to the left (reverse for left-hander). In a closed stance, the right/rear foot is drawn back off the target line, and both feet are aimed slightly to the right (see illustration, below; reverse for left-hander).

Preshot Routine

All golfers should develop a preshot routine, which will keep them focused through the round. If children develop the routine at a young age, it will stay with them throughout their golfing life. Instruct your child to take the following steps in her preshot routine.

1. Look at the target from behind the ball.
2. Pick an intermediate spot on the ground a few feet in front of the ball between the ball and the target.

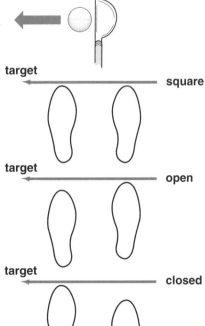

target line

target — **square**

target — **open**

target — **closed**

To practice proper alignment, have the child imagine she is on a railroad track. The ball is on the outer track, which runs to the target, while she stands on the inner track.

The position of a golfer's feet, in square, open, and closed stances.

3. Square the club face to that spot.

4. Align the feet, knees, hips, and shoulders so they're parallel to the target line (a line running from the ball to the target).

5. Feel comfortable in the setup, take one last look at the target, and swing.

Tell your child to use the preshot routine for every part of her game.

Questions and Answers

Q. My child wants to use the overlap grip. Am I wrong in allowing him to use this grip?

A. If he is able to hit the ball using this grip, he can keep using it. But if his hands are too small for him to hold onto the club, he should use the 10-finger grip.

Q. My daughter likes to keep her right/rear hand under the shaft and grip the club in the palm. Should I insist that she cover her left/target thumb?

A. Your daughter may feel she has more control with this grip. If she is very young and she's able to hit the ball, you may leave it. As she gets older, however, she should be able to cover the left thumb. An incorrect grip will only cause problems at a later date.

Q. Is it possible to teach the grip without holding a club?

A. One of the best ways to teach the correct grip is to use a piece of gear called a *grip* (a trainer grip), which is a regular grip used to regrip a club; it can be purchased from your local professional.

Q. My young golfer is always aimed right of the target. How do I correct this?

A. Put two clubs on the ground to form a railroad track, as we described earlier. Get him to set up using these clubs as guides. Once he sees the results, he'll make the necessary adjustments himself.

Q. How tight should my daughter's hold on the club be?

A. She should not grip the club too tightly. Use the analogy of holding a tube of toothpaste: if her grip is too tight, the toothpaste will squirt out. You can also give her a gauge. A tight grip is a 10 and a loose grip is a 1; tell her to grip at a 5 on a scale of 1 to 10. A tight grip causes tension that could spoil a good round.

CHAPTER 5

Putting and Chipping

Most golfers learn the full swing first, on the driving range, but the sense of power that engenders makes it harder for them to transition to a half or a three-quarter swing later on. Although putting, chipping, and pitching are all miniversions of the full swing, it's easier to learn the longer swings (pitching and the full swing) if the golfer has already learned to control the shorter swings (putting and chipping). It's clear, then, that children should always start their golfing experience on the putting green, where they get the combination of feel and touch rather than power.

Fortunately, putting and chipping are fun and fairly easy to learn, which can quickly reward the young beginning golfer with a sense of accomplishment. Your child can play golf every day and not even put a foot on the first tee by playing games on and around the putting green. Since it's imperative that children be skilled at putting and chipping before they go onto a course, they will first need to play for many hours on the green.

Putting and chipping shots don't require strength: they require touch and accuracy. *Putting* is typically the final stage of the game when you play the ball along the putting ground and aim to *hole out* (finish the hole by hitting the ball into the cup) or putt close enough to the cup so you can hole out in the next stroke. The *chip shot* is used when the ball is close to the green, on the *fringe* or *apron* (the area of shorter grass around the green). The goal is to get the ball close to the hole for a tap-in putt—or better still, chip into the hole.

The short game—putting, chipping, and pitching—accounts for about 63 percent of the game; putting alone accounts for over 40 percent of the game. The reason the top players are winning every week is because they are superior to their peers in the area of putting and chipping: not because they strike the ball better and hit it longer.

Keep in mind that the principles for good putting are grip, posture, alignment, and *putting stroke*, the backward and forward motion a golfer makes with the club with the intention of striking the ball.

Teaching Putting

For putting, you'll use, not surprisingly, your putter—the club designed to roll the ball smoothly into the hole. The grip for putting is different than the grip used for the full swing, which is covered in chapter 4.

Grip

There are numerous putting styles and grips, and no one grip is the correct one. Putting, more than any other stroke, requires personal choices: the correct putting grip for your child is the one that feels most comfortable and yields successful results. Have your child experiment with the three basic grips presented here.

The following grips may be adapted for putting. Allow the child to choose the most comfortable grip.

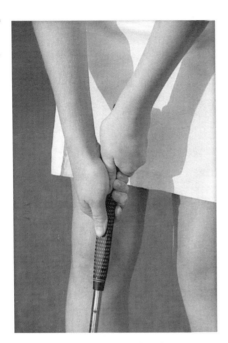

The 10-Finger Putting Grip is the simplest grip for children. The left/target hand is on top, and the right/rear hand is below. Both thumbs go straight down the shaft.

10-Finger Grip for Putting

Most children will use the *10-finger putting grip*, which is slightly different from the full-swing 10-finger grip. These instructions can be used for right- and left-handed players: a right-hander's target side is his left; a left-hander's target side is his right.

Follow these steps for the 10-finger putting grip.

- left/target hand is on top; thumb is down the shaft
- right/rear hand is directly underneath; thumb is down the shaft
- palms face each other
- hands are soft on the grip

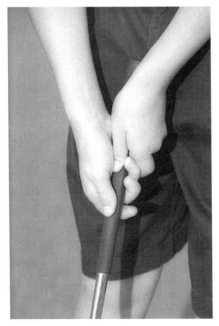

Young golfers can use numerous putting styles and grips. This photograph illustrates the reverse overlap grip for putting.

Reverse Overlap Grip

Follow these steps for the reverse overlap grip.

- left/target hand is on top; thumb is down the shaft
- right/rear hand is below; thumb is down the shaft
- index finger of the left/target hand overlaps the last two fingers of the right/rear hand
- palms face each other
- hands are soft on the grip

Target Hand Below Grip

This grip is identical to the 10-finger grip; just reverse the position of the hands on the club.

- right/rear hand is on the top; thumb is down the shaft
- left/target hand is below; thumb is down the shaft
- palms face each other
- hands are soft on the grip

Posture

As we discussed for grip, use the method that is most comfortable and allows positive results for the child. Some children like to stand erect while others prefer to bend over: both of these positions are correct. But whatever posture the child eventually develops, she should follow these rules. Feet should be shoulder-width apart, with the ball forward of an imaginary line drawn through the center of the stance. The child should bend from the hips so his eyes are over the ball and his arms are hanging freely. His weight should be centered or favoring the left/target side. Visualizing a set of rail-

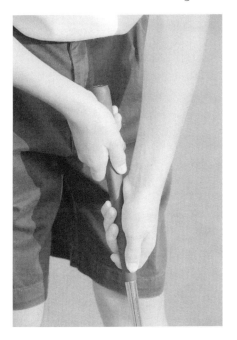 

Left: The target hand below grip is identical to the 10-finger putting grip: you just reverse the position of the hands on the putter.

Right: This young golfer demonstrates proper putting posture.

road tracks is helpful here. The ball sits on the imaginary outer track and the golfer's feet, knees, hips, and shoulders are on the inner track.

Alignment

Teach your child first to aim the putter and then to align her body parallel to the target line. Aiming is simple. Have her stand behind the ball and imagine the outer track of a railroad track running from the ball to the hole.

Have your young golfer emulate this proper putting alignment (note lines).

She can then use that imaginary line from the ball to the hole to aim the putter. Once the putter is aimed, she can then adjust her feet on the imaginary inner track so they're parallel to the target line. Then she can visualize the ball going into the hole.

Stroke

The correct putting stoke doesn't require a big swing. In fact, it's actually quite simple. Swing the club back and through close to the ground. The club, shoulders, and arms move together as a single unit, just like a pendulum, from the *backswing* (swinging the club away from the ball) to the *follow-through* (swinging the club past impact to finish out in front, keeping the legs quiet).

Certain principles reinforce the pendulum stroke. The stroke is made by moving the putter, shoulders, and arms as a unit. The arms and putter form a Y; the putter is the tail of the Y. Move the Y back and through without breaking the shape, which prevents the child from breaking (bending) the wrists. The tail of the Y will always be under the arms (see Y Exercise Drill, page 61). Also emphasize moving the putter equal distances back and through the ball. Accelerate through the ball (Hold in Front of You Drill, page 63). Keep the elbows slightly bent, the posture consistent, and the lower body quiet throughout the swing.

Remember the goal of a putt is to roll the ball into the hole: this does not require a big swing. Rhythm, tempo, and acceleration are very important. The tempo should remain constant, which is easier for golfers to do if they relate the tempo to the constant ticking of a clock.

Speed

It is important to remember that when putting from long distances, distance control or speed of the ball is more important than direction. If the speed of

the ball is too slow, direction is irrelevant: at too slow a speed, the ball will never reach the hole. Use some of the speed drills outlined later in this chapter for distance control.

    In order to increase the distance the ball travels, the golfer must lengthen both the backswing and the follow-through. Have your young golfer practice taking a ball in the right hand and roll it along the green, each time rolling it a little farther than before. Ask her how she was able to make the ball travel farther. If she doesn't guess, show her that she used a longer backswing and a longer follow-through, accelerating through the ball.

In a good putting stroke, the club, shoulders, and arms move together as a single unit—just like a pendulum.

Short Putts and Long Putts

Remind young golfers to keep their lower bodies quiet for all putts, long or short. Their tempo and rhythm also should not vary. The sole difference between a long putt and a short putt is in the length of the backswing and the follow-through. Short putts require a short backswing and follow-through. On the short putts, the golfer should *listen* for the ball falling into the hole, rather than looking up to watch it: most kids miss short putts because they're trying to peek before the follow-through is complete. Longer putts require a longer backswing and follow-through. Tell your stu-

ART

ART is a good mnemonic to remember the three important points on the putting green: acceleration, rhythm, and tempo. *Acceleration* is easily explained in terms of what happens when you start out on a bicycle: the rider starts out slowly and pedals harder to move more quickly. In putting, the backswing is slower than the forward swing. *Rhythm* is the flow of the stroke. *Tempo* can be explained in relation to the ticking of a clock or a metronome: the backswing is the "tick" and the forward swing the "tock."

dents to always accelerate through the ball and keep their heads steady and their eyes over the ball. When you are working on longer putts with your child, initially concentrate more on controlling speed rather than direction.

Uphill Putts and Downhill Putts

The tendency on uphill putts is to leave the ball short of the hole: many golfers never putt hard enough to make the distance. The tempo and rhythm should be the same as for the short and long putts. Have your child grip the putter a little more firmly and accelerate through the ball. Have her visualize an imaginary hole just past the cup and then putt with enough force to get the ball into the imaginary hole.

The tendency on downhill putts is to putt the ball past the hole. The tempo and rhythm should be the same as for the short and long putts. Grip the putter a little lighter and putt the ball toward the toe of the club. Have your child visualize an imaginary hole just short of the cup and putt with just enough force to get the ball into the imaginary hole.

Naturally, the length of the backswing and follow-through will be dictated by the length of the putt. Given uphill and downhill putts of equal distance, the golfer should lengthen the stroke for the uphill and shorten the stroke for the downhill.

Fast and Slow Greens

Help the child determine if the green is *fast* or *slow* by looking at the growth on the green, which is affected by mowing and by weather conditions. Wet greens are always slower than dry greens. If the green appears shiny, the grain is growing away from you and the green is fast. If the green appears dull, the grain is growing toward you and the green is slow. On fast greens, less force is needed to get the ball to the hole. On slow greens, more force is needed to get the ball to the hole.

Have the child watch other players and learn from their putts.

Reading the Green

The green is not always flat; it may have undulations. One of the most impressive golf shots is the putt that appears to be heading off at an angle that seems far from the correct path to the hole; then the putt reaches the top of a slope and makes an arcing turn right into the hole. What a magical shot!

A child can also work toward that kind of magic on the putting green. Always have her check to see how the green slopes. The green may fall to the left or the right. Have her look for the breaks on the green with her eyes, and have her feel the breaks with her feet. Have her imagine that she is pouring a bucket of water on the green, and then watching which direction the water flows.

Children will learn a lot about break by observing their putts. Practicing *breaking putts* (putts that go from right to left or left to right) is a good time for a question-and-answer session. During the practice, ask kids why they thought the ball followed a particular path. This will give them a much clearer understanding of how to play the putt. Show them how to aim off the line to compensate for the slope.

Have your child read the green from behind the ball, from behind the hole, and from the side of the line of the putt. This can be done very quickly and will not slow down play. Remind your child that she should never change her mind about the line of a putt or his stroke while over the ball. She should always visualize the ball going into the hole. Putting accounts for more than 40 percent of the game, so your child should be practicing her putting more than 40 percent of the time! Since the putting stroke is just a miniversion of all the other strokes, all the putting stroke practice on the green contributes to improving the other strokes, as well.

Teaching Chipping

The chip shot is used when the ball is close to the green. It is the shot you use to get the ball over the fringe, land it on the green, and roll it to the hole. Get the ball rolling along the ground as soon as possible around the green. The goal is to get the ball close to the hole for a tap-in putt; better yet, you can chip the ball into the hole.

Chipping is very simple, so have your young golfer approach it like a putt from just off the green. The only difference from putting is the club—use an iron instead of the putter for this shot. Like putting, the chip is about feel and touch. A putter can be used if the fringe is well manicured. Have your child memorize the following tip: putt when you can, chip when you can't putt, and pitch only when you have to.

Golfers can lower their scores drastically simply by improving their chipping, so encourage your child to practice with different clubs from off the green, adapting the same swing with each club. The principles for good chipping are *club selection*, *posture*, *alignment*, and *stroke*.

Club Selection

Club choice is most important for good results. Any club from a pitching wedge to a 5-iron may be the correct choice. The goal is to land the ball on the green and roll it to the hole. The loft on the face of the club will lift the ball over the fringe and onto the green and allow it to roll to the cup. If the flag is near the edge of the green, the club of choice could be a pitching wedge, which would make the ball fly higher and roll less. If the flag is 40 or 50 feet across the green, the club of choice could be a 5- or a 6-iron—the ball will roll farther with these clubs using the same stroke—but a 9- or 7-iron could be used instead. Your child will be able to select the correct club only by improving his stroke and then experimenting with clubs and distances.

Posture

Chipping does not require a big swing. In fact, the chipping stroke is developed from the putting stroke, so the golfer should start with a standard putting posture. Your golfer should grip down the shaft, almost to the metal, *no matter what club is used*. He should adapt the grip used for the full swing.

Here are the basics of a good chip shot. Keep the feet close together, with the stance slightly *open*, that is, with the left/target foot slightly back (see bottom illustration page 49). Bend over at the hips and flex the knees, keeping the weight on the left/target side. As the golfer addresses the ball, his hands should be slightly ahead of the ball, and he should play the ball back in the stance. Ball position in the chip shot stance is very important.

Alignment

Visualizing a railroad track (see pages 48–49), will also help your student with chipping. Have her place the ball on the imaginary outer track. Have her place her feet, knees, hips, and shoulders on the inner track and move her left/target foot back slightly off the line. Her hips and shoulders should be square and her feet slightly open. (See photos, opposite.)

Stroke

The stroke in a chip shot is a pendulum stroke, with the golfer swinging his shoulders, arms, and club back and through. It should be a firm, smooth stroke. Have your student finish with the club out in front and close to the ground, with the weight on the left/target foot. The right/rear knee should go towards the target on the follow-through. This happens when he releases the rear heel on the follow-through.

Tempo and rhythm are most important in chipping, just as they are in putting. Have your child swing the club by using her shoulders and arms, using a pendulum stroke as in putting. Have her keep the hands ahead of the ball throughout the swing. A smooth backswing sets the player up for a smooth stroke. Remind your child that the swing length is the same for each shot: she should change the club for distance.

Have your child imagine that she is standing in a clock with her feet at 6 o'clock and her head at 12 o'clock (see photo, opposite). Then have her make a smooth pendulum swing moving her club from 7 o'clock to 5 o'clock. Have her practice the stroke by always brushing the grass. Here are some basics to remember when you are working with your child on the stroke for a chip shot.

- grip down the shaft, with the hands ahead of the ball
- assume a narrow, open stance, with the weight on the left/target side
- use a pendulum stroke; swing the club back and through to the target

7 o'clock   5 o'clock

6

These four photographs illustrate the chip shot sequence: from top left, the setup, backswing, impact, and follow-through. Note that in the setup, the golfer's hands are ahead of the ball. Imagine the golfer at the center of a clock face. Her backswing reaches back to 7 o'clock; her follow-through runs to 5 o'clock. The clubs on the ground help the golfer with alignment.

Drill Key

 Beginner 6- to 8-year-old

 Beginner 9- to 12-year-old

 Intermediate to Advanced

Warm-Up Drills

Warm-up drills may be used to review the previous lesson or introduce a new concept. Both younger and older children can benefit from a review. Warm-up drills may also be used to get the blood flowing and the mind working. Older children may use a golf club for warm-up drills when appropriate.

Body Awareness: Know your Left and Right Drill

In order to learn how to golf, a child must be able to identify his right and left sides and, eventually, to relate his left side to the target side and his right side to the rear side (reverse this for left-handers). But younger kids sometimes become confused with target and rear labels. Use this drill to help them determine the target and rear sides. Call out instructions, "Show me your left hand and your left foot" and "show me your right hand and your right foot." Once both you and they are confident they have this down pat, introduce the terms "target" and "rear," using the standard phrasing used throughout this book: "left/target" and "right/rear."

Stance: Wide/Narrow, Square, Open/Closed Drill

Have your golfing buddy show you wide, narrow, square, open, and closed stances. She will begin to become familiar with the position of these different stances and the placement of her feet on the ground.

Balance: Ready Position Drill

The *athletic* or *ready position*, where an athlete is in position for play and ready to spring into action, is very similar to the setup for the golf swing. Ask your child to get into an athletic position, just as he would if he were about to return a tennis serve. Then call commands of forward, back, right or left. The child should move to your commands. This is a perfect way to practice balance and weight transfer.

Target Awareness: Big-Ball Drill

Use beach balls, tennis balls, and sponge balls, and have your young golfer hit them to a target. Allow the child to experience success with the larger ball before progressing to the smaller ball. Success is making contact and propelling the ball forward, whether the trajectory is high or low, and the path is right or left of the target. Each child's definition of success is different.

Putting and Chipping Drills

Drills will prove valuable in your teaching. They can be used for positive reinforcement and to develop sound swing fundamentals. In chapters to come are dozens of drills and games to help refine basic skills. The drills in this chapter can be used to practice putting and chipping, and each drill is identified by the golfer's appropriate skill level.

The designations *left/target* and *right/rear* are used so each drill can easily be used for right- and left-handers (remember: the right-hander's target side is the left and rear is the right; the left-hander's target side is the right and rear is the left).

Putting Drills

Grip: A Practice Rhyme Drill

To practice gripping the club correctly, have your young golfers repeat the following rhyme.

> *Grip it in the left,*
> *Then in the right.*
> *Stick your bottom out,*
> *Don't grip it too tight!*

> **Reverse hands for the left-hander**

Grip: Practice without a Club Drill

This drill calls for using a grip only: no club. You will find that without the club, a student will focus more on the grip and her hand position, and not on the swing. Have the student place her left/target hand on the top, and the right/rear hand below. Remind her to keep her hands soft.

Grip: Tight Hands/Soft Hands Drill

Have your child grip and regrip, first with tight hands, then with soft hands. Check that the palms are facing and the thumbs are down the shaft. Give your child a scale he can relate to. Tell your child that a 1 is a loose grip and a 10 is a tight grip. Now, have him grip at a 5.

Pendulum Swing: Y Exercise Drill

Use a grip and tape a huge letter Y onto the grip. Your child should not break the Y; the tail of the Y should always be pointing to the ground. If he breaks (bends) his wrists, the tail will be pointing toward the target. The left/target wrist should remain firm. Tell him to swing his Y back and forth with a little pendulum stroke. The purpose of this drill is to reinforce quiet hands and a shoulder and arm swing.

Pendulum Swing: Use a Putter Drill

Use the putter and remind your student to, "Move the putter back and forth with a little pendulum stroke." The purpose of the drill is to feel the pendulum stroke using a putter.

Y Exercise Drill: using a taped-on Y on the pendulum swing is a good lesson in how the shoulders and arms move as a single unit.

Basic Equipment for Drills

These easy-to-find items will come in handy during drills. All may be used at home and others on a putting green. On a driving range, *only* golf balls may be used.

- **Basketballs or medicine balls.** A weighted ball, such as a basketball or medicine ball, can be used to teach proper setup, backswing, and follow-through. These types of balls are incorporated into several drills in this book. Medicine balls are now made of rubber (forget the old heavy leather ones) and come in a variety of weights.

- **Beach balls.** In early lessons, larger beach balls work great because the larger object makes it easier for new players to make contact. The beach ball can also be used while teaching the proper setup, or keeping the lower body quiet (see photos on page 87).

- **Cones.** Cones are great as targets. If you are teaching a group, they can also be used to divide kids safely at different stations.

- **Golf balls.** I hardly need to say that you'll need a lot of these!

- **Grips.** Used for regripping clubs, grips are perfect for teaching kids grip and swing basics. Children would be more inclined to swing with a club in their hands; using only a grip, they will be able to concentrate more on your instructions. Many golf pro shops sell club grips; they generally cost $3 to $4.

- **Hula hoops.** These work well as targets.

- **Impact bags.** Impact bags, a cloth bag that you can fill with soft material such as towels or sheets, help reinforce body position at the point of impact, when the golfer's club comes in contact with the ball. These bags can be used in conjunction with a mirror.

- **Lobby brooms.** A broom with a short handle (about $1\frac{1}{2}$ feet long) can help reinforce proper swing techniques without the worry of causing injury.

- **Metronome.** A metronome, a device used in music teaching to mark time by means of regularly recurring ticks or flashes, can be used to teach proper tempo for putting, chipping, or the full swing.

- **Mirrors.** Full-length mirrors are useful for feedback on a golfer's grip, posture, and alignment. Small mirrors may be purchased from your local pro (see photo on page 84).

- **Paddles.** Paddles, such as table tennis paddles, help you reinforce proper swing techniques and can help you illustrate the importance of keeping the club face square at impact.

- **Rubber or sponge balls.** Soft rubber balls (the size of a tennis ball) may be substituted for golf balls, initially. The larger ball is easier to hit.

- **Tennis balls.** Tennis balls may be substituted for golf balls initially.

- **Two-by-fours.** Lengths of two-by-fours can be used to teach proper alignment. You can use them to create the railroad track discussed earlier. Placing two clubs on the ground will also work for the railroad track.

- **Weighted clubs.** Swinging one of these will help you teach proper tempo.

- **Whiffle balls.** Golf whiffle balls are good for practice: you can work on swing technique in your backyard or indoors without worrying about broken windows!

Pendulum Swing: Hold in Front of You Drill

Use the putter and repeat, "Swing back and through and hold the putter in front of you." The purpose of the drill is to emphasize that the child accelerates through the ball and doesn't stop at the ball.

Pendulum Stroke: One-Arm Drill

Using a pendulum stroke, have your student swing the club in the left/target hand, and then in the right/rear hand. Putt with the left/target hand only, then putt with the right/rear hand only. Do not break (bend) the wrist. This emphasizes how the shoulders and arms work as a unit.

Pendulum Swing and Swing Path: Make a Pathway Drill

Place two clubs on the ground, approximately a club head apart. Have your young golfer set the putter head between the clubs and make pendulum strokes. The purpose of this drill is to correct swing motion and swing path. If your child uses his hands instead of his shoulders and arms to putt, he will hit the clubs on the ground with the head of the putter on the backswing or on the follow-through.

Alignment: Make a Railroad Track Drill

Make a railroad track by placing two clubs on the ground and placing a ball in the middle. Set up to the hole, and have your child align his body parallel to the nearer club, the imaginary inner track. The purpose of the drill is to help the student set up to the ball and parallel his body to the target line.

Make a Railroad Track Drill.

Distance: Yardstick Drill

Mark a yardstick at 1-inch intervals. Place it on the ground, in front of your golfer, and pick one mark as your center point. Have your golfer practice her swing length with her club only, using the yardstick as a guide to her swing length. Then introduce the ball, and place it at your center point. Have your child put her club head at the center point and make swings of different lengths. Swing 1–1, then 2–2, then 3–3: if the backswing is 1 inch, the ball should travel 1 foot; with a backswing of 2 inches, the ball will travel 2 feet; etc.. The purpose of this drill is to relate

Above: Yardstick Drill.

Right: The Ladder Drill will help your golfer achieve different distances.

swing length to the distance that the ball travels.

Distance: Cluster Drill

Place four balls on the green. Have your child putt the first ball making a 3-3 swing length. Then have her putt the next three balls to the spot where the original ball stopped. The purpose of the drill is to stop all the balls in a cluster and relate swing length to distance.

Distance: Ladder Drill

Place four strings on the green, spaced about a club length apart. Place four balls behind the first string. Have your child putt the first ball past the last (fourth) string. Putt the second ball past the third string. Putt the third ball past the second string, and finally putt the last ball past the first string. The purpose of this drill is to make different swings for different distances. Tees may be substituted for the strings. But visually, strings are a better teaching tool.

Speed and Direction: Putting to Different Targets Drill

Place four balls in one central spot. Then have your student putt these to different targets on the green. You can use tees for targets, or even putt to the fringe. The purpose of the drill is to work on distance and direction.

Feel: Roll Drill

Have your child stand on the green with a golf ball in his right hand. Have him roll the ball to the target. The purpose of the drill is to create a feeling of roll, without using the putter. Just instruct him to step forward and release the ball low to the ground.

The left-hander will practice this drill using her left hand.

Also ask the child to relate putting and chipping to working with paints or playing a musical instrument: the softness of the flute or a violin can compare to the feel of putting.

Feel: Closed Eyes Drill

First, have your child practice the putting stroke with his eyes closed. He should set up to a ball, then close his eyes. He puts the ball, putting the remaining three balls with closed eyes. All the balls should finish at the same spot. The purpose of this drill is to create feel.

Feel: 3-Second Drill

Have your child practice her putting stroke, looking at the target only. When she feels that she is making the correct swing for that distance putt, have her putt looking at the ball only. She must putt within 3 seconds. The purpose of this drill is to learn to react to the target.

Short Putts: Line Drill

Place five balls in a straight line, spacing each successive ball farther from the hole. Have your child putt the ball closest to the hole first. Then have her move away from the target to putt the second ball, third ball, etc. Let her putt all five balls. If a ball is not holed out, start again. She shouldn't peek—which on a short putt would involve moving the head before the follow-through is complete—*listening* instead for the ball to drop into the hole. The purpose of this drill is to develop a compact stroke and build confidence for short putts.

Line Drill: making these short putts in a line will help your child develop a compact stroke and build confidence.

Short Putts: Circle Drill

Place five balls in a circle around the cup, about a putter's length from the cup. Have students putt each ball into the hole. The purpose of this drill is to develop a compact stroke for short putts and to build confidence. Remember, success breeds confidence. Continue to move the circle farther away from the hole after each successful attempt at the drill.

Chipping Drills

Grip: 25 Grips a Day Drill

Have your child grip and regrip at least 25 times each day. Adapt the grip from the fundamentals: the 10-finger, interlock, or overlap grip (see pages 45–46). The purpose of this drill is to reinforce the correct grip. This drill may be practiced indoors with a grip only.

The Toss or Roll Drill will help a young golfer identify the ball flight of a chip shot.

Roll: Toss or Roll Drill

Have your student stand a few feet off the green, facing the green, and bend down low. She takes a ball in the right hand and, releasing the ball low, rolls it toward the target (reverse the hand for left-hander). The ball will be in the air for a few feet and will then roll along the green. Instruct her to get the ball rolling as quickly as possible. The purpose of this drill is to identify the ball flight of the chip shot. The flight has very little time in the air but a lot of roll time. ① → ②

Stroke: Brush the Grass Drill

Have your student brush the grass with his club head making 7 to 5 o'clock swings. In order to chip successfully, your child must be able to brush the grass during the practice swings. He will receive good feedback from the grass: if he's able to brush the grass, he'll be able to make crisp contact with the ball. The purpose of the drill is to develop a firm stroke using good tempo and rhythm. ① → ③

Stroke: Y Drill

Have your students repeat this rhyme: "Swing the club back and through and hold it in front of you." Or, using the grip with the Y taped onto it (see photo page 61), have them follow this rhyme: "Swing your Y back and through and hold it in front of you." Or, "Swing your Y back and forth with a little pendulum stroke." The purpose of this drill is to help create a pendulum stroke with the shoulders and arms and to eliminate the scooping action of the wrists. ①

Tempo: Metronome Drill

Set the metronome on 64 or 65. Use the tempo to practice miniswings. Then practice the chipping stroke accompanied by the metronome (the metronome can also be used for putting practice). The purpose of the drill is to develop a stroke with consistent tempo. ① → ③

Swing Length: Tee or Yardstick Drill

Place a yardstick on the target line, or place two tees in the ground on the target line. The yardstick should be marked for a 7 to 5 o'clock swing length; if you are using tees, set them up about 2 feet apart, 1 foot on either side of the ball. If using a yardstick, mark it at 0 and at 24 inches.

Have your student make practice swings beside the tees or the yardstick. The purpose of the drill is to help visually identify the length of the swing for all chips. The swing length will always be the same, regardless of the distance; the choice of club will change. ⚑ → ⚑

Arms and Shoulder Swing: Active Hands Drill

Have the child grip the club in the normal manner and set up for a chip shot in the correct manner. Extend the shaft of the club upward by tapping a yardstick (you can also use a broken shaft) to the club grip. Have the child do a chip shot. If the extended shaft hits the left/target side of the golfer, his wrists are too active. Continue to swing until he eliminates the wrist action. He will receive feedback from the extended shaft. The purpose of the drill is to help keep the hands ahead of the club head and eliminate a scooping action. ⚑ → ⚑

The Active Hands Drill will help a golfer keep his hands ahead of the club head and eliminate a scooping action.

Follow-Through: Weight on the Target Side Drill

Set your golfer up on the left/target foot. Have her move her right/rear foot back so she is only resting on the toe of the right/rear foot. Have her make chips from this position. This drill sets the player up so she starts with the weight on the left/target side and finishes with the weight on the left/target side. The purpose of the drill is to emphasize a quiet lower body with the weight always favoring the left/target side. ⚑ → ⚑

Path and Alignment: Track Drill

Place two clubs on the ground, with the clubs pointing toward the target and parallel to each other. The clubs re-create the railroad track; place the ball between the clubs, close to the outer club, and position the ball so it's back in the stance of your golfer. Have your golfer parallel her feet, knees, hips, and shoulders to the nearer club. Move her left/target foot back off the line. Have her play chips to a target. The purpose of the drill is to help identify an incorrect swing path and alignment. ⚑ → ⚑

Club Selection: Three-Tee Drill

Place three tees on the green at different distances from the fringe. Have your golfer set up just off the green, as if he were setting up for a chip.

Then let him experiment with different clubs to identify the ideal club to use to reach each tee using a 7 to 5 o'clock, or 1–1 foot, swing length. Have him use the same swing length with each club. Each club should roll the ball a different distance. The purpose of the drill is to relate club selection to distance.

Direction and Speed: Target Drill

Set up three targets on the green. Practice greens have 9 holes. Use the holes as the target for more advanced players and use a large circle or hula hoops for the beginners. Use 21 balls to chip to the targets. Set up off the green, as you would for the chip shot. Alternate every chip between short, medium, and long chips. Set the goal to suit the skill level of your child. The goal may be to chip 3 balls into each hole, or to chip 3 balls into each circle or hoop. When the 21 balls have been used up, check your golfer's 7 to 5 o'clock swing and tempo. The purpose of the drill is to emphasize speed and direction for good results.

Getting the Ball Up and Down: Chip and Hole Out Drill

Have your golfer chip to different holes, then go onto the green and use the putter to putt the ball into the hole. The goal is to have her chip the ball close enough so she can hole out in one putt. The purpose of the drill is to get all chips in or close to the hole.

Using the Loft on the Face of the Club to Get the Ball Airborne: Golf Bag Drill

Lay a golf bag down on the fringe of the green and position it between the player and the target. Have the child chip, leading with her hands; the club face will lift the ball over the bag and onto the green. The purpose of the drill is to demonstrate that when the hands lead, the ball will lift over the fringe and roll to the hole. Never leave a golf bag near the green on the course. This is a practice drill for the practice green or the driving range.

The Golf Bag Drill will help a golfer see that when the hands lead, the ball will lift over the fringe and roll to the hole. Remember that you should never leave a golf bag near the green when playing on the course; this is a drill for the practice green.

Pendulum Stroke: Two-Club Drill

Have your golfer set up with a club in each hand: a pitching wedge in one and a 9-iron in the other (you can substitute golf grips for the clubs in this drill). Have her make pendulum strokes. The clubs should be moving in unison. If the club heads hit each other, her hands are active. The purpose of the drill is to help create the stroke with the shoulders and arms, keeping the hands quiet. 🏌️1 → 🏌️3

Pendulum Stroke: One-Arm Swings

Have your golfer chip balls from off the green using only one arm. Set up with the club in the left/target hand, then chip balls onto the green using only the left/target arm. Then set up with the club in the right/rear hand, then chip balls onto the green using only the right/rear hand. This drill will help develop the right feeling for using the arms and shoulders as a unit. 🏌️2 → 🏌️3

Understanding When to Use the Pendulum Stroke: Rhyme Drill

This rhyme will help your golfer understand when to use the pendulum stroke. Have your child memorize this verse. 🏌️1

> We move from the green and onto the fringe,
> This is where chipping begins.
> Change the club but not the stroke,
> Continue with a little pendulum stroke.

Putting and Chipping Games

Kids love to play minigames, which can be played alone, with Mom or Dad, or with a friend. In the beginning, don't keep score. When the kids are ready to keep score and compete, they will let you know. Kids are also very creative and they will invent their own games. You can also modify these putting and chipping games so you can play them indoors. Use soft balls (soft, as in texture) for chipping.

Minigames that you can play both on and around the green are also the perfect way to learn about good sportsmanship. This is where your child learns to win and lose graciously.

Putting Games
Around the World Game

Place ten balls in a circle, 1 foot from the cup. Have your golfer putt the balls into the cup. After holing out all ten balls, move the balls 2 feet from the cup. Continue moving the balls away from the hole in 1-foot increments. The goal is to hole out all ten balls from 8 to 10 feet.

Putt until 10 Drop Game

Place ten balls in a line, spaced at 1-foot intervals. Have your child putt all ten balls into the hole. The game is won when all balls have been holed out. If one ball is missed, replace all the balls and begin again.

Attack the Hole Game

Draw a 2-foot circle around the hole. Use a string or talcum powder to draw the circle. If you are using talcum powder, get permission from the professional. Set up 10 to 20 feet away. Each golfer earns 1 point for a ball in the circle and 2 points for a ball in the hole. Practice with five to ten balls.

Over the Finish Line Game

Place a 10-foot string across the green. Set up about 20 feet away from the string. The goal is to putt each ball over the line. Each golfer earns 1 point for every ball that finishes past the line; subtract 1 point for every ball that lands short of the line.

Build a Golf Hole Game

In this game, your young golfer uses materials prepared at home to build a miniature dogleg or a par-5 hole on the practice putting green—be sure to check with the golf pro, course superintendent, or club manager first for permission!—or at home in a garage or backyard.

To define the teeing ground, the child can use a pair of colored golf balls pasted to tees. He lines both sides of the fairway and outlines the out-of-bounds area and water hazards with additional tees. The child then wraps bright tape around them to connect them (use the nonsticky fluorescent tape available in hardware stores). Branches and twigs can represent the rough, and plastic lids represent sand in a bunker.

If this is a backyard or garage, the child can define the green with kitchen twine, using a small paper cup for the hole.

Ask him to identify the parts of the hole and explain to you the rules for out-of-bounds and hazards. This is a great way to teach the rules. Be sure to have the child collect all the materials after the game for use another time.

Chipping Games

Over the String Game

Tie a 5-foot string between two 6-inch rulers. Place them in the ground, just off the green. Have your golfer chip the ball over the string. Score 1 point for every ball chipped over the string; subtract 1 point for every ball chipped under the string. Instruct the child to make a 7 to 5 o'clock swing length.

Long and Short Game

Set up two circular targets at different distances. Use string or talcum powder (again, if you have the pro's permission). Have your golfer make a 7 to 5 o'clock swing length (or 1–1 foot if using a yardstick), using different clubs to achieve each distance and reach each target. Adjust the diameter of the target area as your child's skill level improves. Score 2 points for every ball that finishes at the target. Modify the game for less-skilled children.

Hole-in-One Game

If your golfing buddy is quite proficient, have her chip to the same hole until one shot is holed out.

Modify the game for less-skilled players by limiting the attempts to 20 balls: the golfer receives 3 points for a hole in one and 1 point for a shot within 1 foot of the cup.

Up and Down Game

The golfer plays 9 holes on the practice green from the fringe. Since there are 9 holes, the golfer should approach the hole from 9 different positions on the fringe. Play to different targets, using a 7 to 5 o'clock swing length (a 1–1 foot swing length) and the appropriate club for the distance. Go onto the green and use the putter to finish out the hole. The goal is to chip the ball close enough so you can hole out in one putt.

Kangaroo Ball

Place a ball on the green at least one club length from the fringe. Have your golfer chip from off the green, using a predetermined number of balls. The goal is for your golfer to land her ball on the ball on the green.

Questions and Answers

Q. My young golfing buddy works very hard during her putting lesson, but she always wants to hit balls after the lesson. Should I allow her to?

A. Provided you have set goals, and she has reached them during the lesson, go ahead and allow her to hit a few balls. But, bearing in mind that her lesson was on putting and not on the full swing, allow her to hit balls *without* instruction.

Q. My 7-year-old son always wants to play from the white tees with me. Should I let him join me?

A. Letting your 7-year-old join you on the white tees may be fine, occasionally. But it will slow up play, and the lengthening of the fairway will not help his game. Tell him that as soon as he can shoot par from the 100-yard mark, he can move back to 150 yards. From there, he can move to the forward tees. Make him a scorecard for the 100-yard mark so he feels more like he's playing "for real."

Q. My 6-year-old tires quickly and wants to stop after a few holes. Should I insist she continue?

A. No 6-year-old is capable of playing even a 9-hole course. Even if kids in this age group play from the 100-yard mark, they may only make it to the third or fourth hole before pooping out.

Q. My 12-year-old golfing buddy always cries when he loses. He always makes excuses for his bad shots and never credits his playing partner's good play. What should I do?

A. Losing is a learning experience and a growing experience. Your friend will not be receptive to criticism after a bad round, but let him know that there will always be winners and losers. How he deals with winning and losing is important: it takes more character to be a gracious loser than a gracious winner. Bring up the positive things in his round and forget the negative. Remind him that everyone has some bad shots, and there is no need to make excuses. His playing partner deserves credit for playing well. Make sure your friend understands that his golf score does not reflect who he is as a person.

Q. My daughter has done very well in practice, but she has decided that she doesn't want to play in any tournaments. What should I do?

A. Continue to allow her to practice, since she *is* enjoying it. Respect her choice and don't push her into competition. Her decision may be a result of feeling pressure from you or her peers; she may also fear failure; or maybe she just feels that golf is fun when it's not competitive. Continue to praise and nurture her, and of course keep playing golf with her!

Q. My son played a great first tournament, and after the round, he was shouting and jumping about. I was pleased that he was excited, but how much celebrating after a win is "too much"?

A. It is good to be happy, but your son must respect his opponent. He must shake hands and thank him for a great game.

Q. My young golfing buddy is way below the standard of his peers: he works very hard, but he doesn't show any improvement on the course.

A. He should continue to practice and play, provided he's enjoying the game. Some kids take a little more time to mature in the game. If he continues with a good work ethic, he will reap the rewards eventually.

CHAPTER 6

Pitching and the Full Swing

In my experience, teaching the pitch shot is the most difficult lesson because most golfers have started out on the driving range instead of on the putting green and therefore find it difficult to transition to the shorter swing. It's important for your young golfing buddy to have learned putting and chipping (see chapter 5) before attempting pitching and the full swing.

Pitch Shot

The pitch shot is considered an *approach shot* to the green. Golfers should play the pitch shot only when there is an obstacle, such as a bunker or a pond, between them and the green. The goal for pitching is accuracy, not distance. A good pitch shot will get the ball in the air quickly, with a high trajectory.

The pitch shot has more airtime and less roll than the chip, and it should be executed with a sand wedge or a pitching wedge. Most sets of clubs for juniors include either a 9-iron or a pitching wedge. Young golfers should use the 9-iron, which is the next most lofted club in the bag, if they don't have a pitching or sand wedge. The wedges have the most loft on the face, which causes the ball to have a higher trajectory—and height is necessary for a pitch shot.

The principles for the basic pitch shot are grip, setup, alignment, and the swing.

Grip

Have your child adapt the basic fundamental 10-finger grip from chapter 4. Grip a little down the shaft for a shorter distance; grip toward the top for a longer distance. The longer the shaft, the farther the ball will go. By gripping down on the shaft, the child will have more control and the ball won't travel as far as it otherwise would.

Setup and Alignment

The setup for the pitch shot is similar to that of the chip shot, except you should have your golfer use a slightly wider stance. The stance is slightly open, with the left/target foot pulled slightly back off the target line. Just as you would for the chip shot, have your child bend at the hips, with knees flexed and eyes over the ball. Hips and shoulders are square. For this shot, the ball is centered in the stance. The weight favors the left/target side, with about 60 percent of the weight on the left/target side. As you would do in a chip shot, keep your hands ahead of the ball and toward the inseam of the left/target pant leg.

Swing

In this section, I walk you through the pitch shot swing with your student. Have your child swing to a waist-high height on the backswing and to waist high on the follow-through. Her hands should go to the waist-high level. In her setup, her shoulders and arms should form a triangle. As her shoulders turn away from the target, the triangle she's formed and the club move as a unit. Have her point her thumbs to the sky at waist height in the backswing. Have her move the right/rear knee toward the target on the downswing and finish with her thumbs to the sky on the follow-through. Remind her that, as she turns her shoulders, the club swings upward.

The downswing should resemble an underarm toss of the ball to a target. The body weight favors the left/target side and remains there throughout the swing. She should finish with her weight on the left/target side.

Here again, you can have the child imagine she is standing in front of a clock face, with her feet at 6 o'clock and her head at 12 o'clock. Her swing in the pitch shot is from 9 o'clock to 3 o'clock: she swings until her hands reach 9 o'clock on the backswing and 3 o'clock on the follow-through.

Your child should remember these simple pitching instructions as she practices this shot.

- set up with the feet open and slightly wider than for the chip
- set up with the weight on the left/target side; keep the lower body quiet on the backswing
- thumbs to the sky, thumbs to the sky (or, thumbs to the sky at waist high)
- hold the finish with weight on the left/target side

Full Swing

The full swing is executed with the woods and irons; this is the power swing, the one used to hit the ball a long distance. Nonetheless, the full swing is an extension of the chip and pitch shots. The swing is a series of

9 o'clock

3 o'clock

The pitch shot. On an imaginary clock face, the golfer's hands will be at 9 o'clock on the backswing and 3 o'clock on the follow-through.

coordinated movements: turning away from the ball, and returning to and through the ball in sequence. The full swing requires the same tempo and rhythm for all clubs, from the driver to the sand wedge.

The principles of the full swing are the grip, posture, alignment, and the swing.

Grip

The 10-finger, interlock, or overlap grip may be used. For the 10-finger grip, the child places the club in the left/target hand, with the club's grip running diagonally across the hands in the palm and fingers. He then closes his hand around the grip, feeling grip pressure in the last three fingers of the left/target hand. The left/target thumb rests on the inside of the shaft. The

This young golfer demonstrates a great swing: the proper position at impact (above) and a wonderful follow-through (below).

left/target thumb and index finger form a V that points between his chin and right/rear shoulder. The grip of the club rests beneath the heel pad of the left/target hand.

He then places the right/rear hand on the club, holding it in the fingers, with the right/rear thumb resting on the left/target side of the shaft. The lifeline of the right/rear hand fits snugly over the left/target thumb. The index fingers and thumbs of both hands form a V that points between the chin and the right/rear shoulder. Two to three knuckles are visible on the left/target hand.

A soft grip pressure is essential. Place emphasis on the correct grip, as this is the only way the child can square the club face to the ball.

Posture

The golfer's posture, the position of the feet and body as he sets up to the ball, remains constant for all clubs. The only variation from sand wedge to driver is the distance the golfer stands from the ball and the ball position in the stance.

The woods require a slightly wider stance. The length of the shaft dictates the distance you stand from the ball. For example, when you use your driver, you stand farther away from the ball than you would with your pitching wedge (the shaft of the driver is longer than the shaft of the pitching wedge). All clubs decrease in ½-inch increments from the driver to the pitching wedge.

The ball position also varies. As the shaft length increases the ball position is moved gradually forward of center toward the left/target heel. For example, the ball should be at the center of the stance for the pitching wedge and off the left/target heel for the driver.

Have your child set up with his feet shoulder-width apart. His weight should be distributed about 50/50 from left to right and from heel to toe. Have him bend over from the hips and tilt his upper body slightly to the right/rear. For a right-hander, the right/rear shoulder will be lower than the left/target shoulder and the right/rear hand will be lower than the left/target hand (reverse for a left-hander). There will be a slight weight adjustment

pitching wedge   5-iron   driver

Club length dictates the distance a golfer must stand from the ball at setup. Notice the variation in shaft length between the wood and the irons.

with the driver, with more weight on the right/rear side than the left/target side. This is the result of the ball being forward in a wide stance.

Alignment

Have your child align his feet, knees, hips, and shoulders parallel to the target line. Again, visualizing a railroad track will help here. The ball is on the imaginary outer track; the feet, knees, hips, and shoulders are on the inner track.

Swing

There are two parts to the full swing: the backswing and the downswing or forward swing. During the backswing, the shoulders and arms swing the club and the body follows. During the downswing or forward swing, the lower body leads, which allows the arms, hands, right/rear shoulder, and club to follow through to the finish. On the backswing, the upper body coils over the right/rear leg. On the downswing or forward swing, the golfer shifts his weight to the left/target leg and the upper body uncoils. (Target and rear designations are used so you can easily adapt these instructions for both right- and left-handers.)

Remember that in order to swing a golf club, the body needs to be free of tension. Most children are normally tension-free—unless parents give them too much to think about! Following are more detailed explanations of the backswing and downswing, followed by some simple instructions to share with your child.

The full swing, from address to backswing, through impact and follow-through.

Backswing

Have your child set up to the ball free of tension, feeling light on his feet. A light grip is essential. Explain grip to the child as being on a scale of 1 to

10: 1 is a loose grip and 10 is a tight grip. Have him grip the club at a 5. Grip pressure should remain the same throughout the swing.

The triangle formed by the shoulders and arms at address must be maintained throughout the swing (#1). Have him move the club away from the ball using the left/target shoulder, arms, hands, and club. They should move together as a unit. The head of the club moves away from the ball and remains close to the ground for the first 12 inches. Do not let him cock his wrists: the wrists remain quiet. His weight should begin to move to the inside of the right/rear leg, which remains flexed.

The turn of the shoulders creates the swing. The shoulder turn allows the club to move naturally backward and upward. The club face on the takeaway remains square in relation to the body. When your golfer has the club halfway back, the club is parallel to the ground with the toe of the club pointing to the sky. The weight is on the inside of the right/rear leg, which remains flexed. The shoulder, arms, and club have remained in front of the chest. The head has moved slightly to the right/rear, while the eyes remain watching the ball. The lower body remains quiet throughout the backswing(#2).

The right/rear elbow bends, and the target arm is parallel to the ground. The club and the arms form an L-shape as the club begins to move upward. The left/target arm should remain straight, not locked. At the top of the backswing, the left/target hand is flat (square) and in line with the left/target forearm. The right/rear elbow is pointing toward the ground. The club is pointing toward the target. At the top of the backswing, the left/target shoulder is also behind the ball, with the head moved slightly to the right/rear. Do not try to keep the head directly over the ball: keeping the head still causes swing problems. The weight is on the inside of the right/rear leg, which remains flexed. The body stays in posture throughout the swing(#3).

The backswing creates a problem for most golfers, because there is too much leg movement. A good check is to remind them they are not hitting the ball with the backswing: they're swinging the club in balance to put themselves in a good athletic position.

Downswing or Forward Swing

The downswing or forward swing is initiated with the lower body. The weight moves to the left/target foot, and the hips move laterally toward the target. Tell your golfer to remain centered. The right/rear knee points toward the ball. The hands drop close to the right/rear hip, retaining the angle between the club and arms, the hips are turning. The shoulders are uncoiling and catching up to the legs and hips. At impact, the club face is square and the club shaft is in line with the back of the left/target hand. The right/rear shoulder and club head arrive at impact at the same time. The hips are turned, and the shoulders are slightly open.

The weight is on the left/target foot, and the right/rear heel has released slightly from the ground. The head is behind the ball (photo #4, page 79).

The follow-through is the swing through the ball: the body has turned through the ball (photo #5). The left/target arm begins to bend, and the right/rear arm extends. This is a mirror image of the backswing. The right/rear arm rotates over the left/target arm, allowing the head to follow the ball. The shaft points upward.

The majority of the weight is on the left/target side, with the right/rear knee pointing toward the target: the right/rear foot is on the toe. The hips and shoulders are turned fully, and the right/rear shoulder should be closer to the target than the left/target shoulder. The arms and hands finish over the left/target shoulder, and the club is behind the head. This is a balanced finish (photo #6).

The swing is basically a coil of the upper body followed by a shift to the right/rear, a shift to the target and uncoil, and then a hold of the finish. You can simplify the move for your child by using any of the following directions.

- swing the club over the right/rear shoulder, then swing it over the left/target shoulder
- coil and uncoil your upper body
- turn and return
- swing back and through

Club face positions.

square

closed

open

- weight on the right/rear foot and weight on the left/target foot
- back to the target; tummy to the target

Ball Flight

Now that you have progressed through the different shots your child will need on the golf course, let's look at *error detection*, that is, trying to figure out why shots fly off the club in unexpected and unintended directions. Error detection is something best left to your teaching professional. However, a basic understanding of what causes a ball to behave the way it does will help you understand how intricate and nuanced the game truly is.

The two most important factors that affect how a ball will fly off the club follow.

- **Path.** The swing path on which the club head travels, from the top of the backswing through impact, will influence the initial direction the ball will travel.

- **Face.** The position of the face of the club at impact will dictate whether the ball ends up on the target, or to the right or left of the target. The club face position at impact affects both the distance and the direction of the ball.

Swing Path

Swing path refers to the path the club head travels, from the top of the back-swing through impact. This path will determine the direction of the ball. There are three paths: an *in-to-in* swing path, an *out-to-in* swing path, and an *in-to-out* swing path. Each pattern is described below.

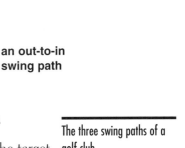

an in-to-in swing path

an in-to-out swing path

an out-to-in swing path

- **In-to-in swing path.** The club travels from inside the target line on the downswing, to square at impact, to back inside the target line on the follow-through. With this swing path, the ball begins its journey on target.

- **Out-to-in swing path.** The club travels from outside the target line on the downswing, to square at impact, to inside the target

Common Beginner Problems

Almost all beginners will experience some, if not all, of the following problems. Don't worry. You'll find drills in this chapter to help young golfers avoid them all.

Topping

A *topped ball* is a ball that is struck above the ball center or equator, usually resulting in a ball that dribbles only a short distance. Beginners do not have a very good picture in their minds of the golf swing, so they try to "help" the ball into the air. They do this by hanging back on the right/rear side and trying to scoop the ball into the air. Instruct your child to initiate the downswing with the large muscles of the lower body. Another problem that leads to a topped ball is an up-and-down movement in the swing, rather than the turn-and-return or coil-and-uncoil movement of the body. The golfer has a tendency to move his body up and down. Tension and a tight grip can also cause a topped ball.

A topped ball can also result from an out-to-in swing path. A golf club shipping box can be used to help you determine if this is the problem. Have your child set up parallel to a golf club box; place the ball beside the box and have him swing. If his swing path is out-to-in, his club will strike the top of the box.

Hitting Behind the Ball

When a golfer hits behind the ball, she is striking the area behind the ball instead of hitting the ball first and then taking a divot after striking the ball. The golfer's tendency is to *throw the club head at the ball*. To do that, the player takes the club away with her hands, rather than making a full shoulder turn. The left / target arm collapses at the top of the backswing, which causes the club to go past parallel. The player then basically throws the club at the ball.

Have your child practice staying in posture, coiling and uncoiling. Practice miniswings (the 7 to 5 o'clock swing, the 8 to 4 o'clock swing, and the 9 to 3 o'clock swing). Have her put a tee in the ground a few inches behind the ball and extend to take the club away over the tee using the left/target shoulder and arms to initiate the takeaway. When the player takes the club away with the hands only, there is a tendency to leave the weight on the left/target side at the top of the backswing. The weight then moves back to the right/rear side on the downswing, causing the club to hit the ground before the ball.

The player may also be dropping her right/rear shoulder on the downswing. Promote the feeling of turning the shoulders level. Drop the hands and retain the angle between the arms and the club shaft. Keep the shoulders level. Have her practice the baseball drill outlined in this chapter (see page 88), and then set up for her golf swing: she will notice that she no longer hits the ground behind the ball.

Shank or Socket

A *shank*, also known as a *socket*, is a word that golfers hate to hear. The *hosel* (the part of the club that joins the club head to the shaft) rather than the club face strikes the ball. The ball shoots out to the right (to the left for a left-hander). I prefer to call this a *lateral*; for some reason, that word does not seem to play with the mind as much as *shank* or *socket* does! This shot has numerous causes.

- The shank may be caused by an out-to-in or an in-to-out swing path. To promote the correct swing path, practice with two clubs on the ground, similar to the railroad track (see top illustration page 49). Place the clubs parallel to one another; have your golfer set up parallel to the clubs and make practice swings. He should avoid hitting the outside club. This will promote an in-to-in swing path. To eliminate an out-to-in swing path, place two balls on the ground, side by side, about 1 inch apart. Have your golfer make swings and aim to hit the inside ball.

- Moving the upper body ahead of the ball on the downswing may also cause a shank or a socket. Have your child concentrate on keeping the body centered on the downswing. Practice swinging the club with the feet together.

- The shank or socket is also a result of too much weight towards the toes in the setup. Place a golf ball under the toes of each foot, then have your child make practice swings.

- Rolling the club face open on the takeaway or backswing could also result in a shank or socket. Have your child make swings keeping the back of the left/target hand to the target on the takeaway.

- Too tight a grip and tension in the golf swing causes this ugly lateral. Have your child set up and inhale and exhale before the swing to release all that tension.

Whiff or Fresh Air

Beginners suffer from this shot. A *whiff*, also known as *fresh air*, is when a golfer swings and completely misses the ball. Whiffs count as a stroke! This miss is caused by inexperience, not understanding either the swing or the basic fundamentals. Practice grip, posture, and alignment, and have the child remain in posture throughout the swing. Don't let him move his head up and down. Have him practice miniswings and have him keep his eyes on the ball. He should make 7 to 5 o'clock swings until he consistently makes contact with the ball, then increase swing length to 8 and 4 o'clock and finally 9 and 3 o'clock.

line on the follow-through. With this swing path, the ball begins its journey left of the target.

- **In-to-out swing path.** The club travels from inside the target line on the downswing, to square at impact, to outside the target line on the follow-through. With this swing path, the ball begins its journey right of the target.

Pitching and Full-Swing Drills

On the following pages are a handful of drills and games you can use to work with your young golfing buddy on the full swing and the pitch shot. Each one is geared to a specific skill level. Target and rear designations are used so these drills are immediately understandable for both right- and left-handers (a right-hander's target side is her left; a left-hander's target side is her right).

Don't stop with the exercises on these pages: have fun, be creative, and make up your own drills!

Posture: Mirror Drill #1

Set up in front of a full-length mirror and have your young golfers recite this rhyme.

> Grip it in the left,
> Then in the right.
> Stick your bottom out
> And tilt to the right.

Mirror Drill #2. Observing their posture in a mirror for feedback helps young golfers build the foundation for a good athletic position.

The purpose of this drill is to reinforce proper grip and posture.

Posture: Mirror Drill #2

Have your golfer stand tall and bend at the hips, with knees flexed. Have her tilt the upper body to the right/rear, with the right/rear shoulder slightly lower than the left/target shoulder. Observe the posture in the mirror for feedback. The purpose of the drill is to build the foundation for a good athletic position (see photo, left).

Grip: Use-a-Grip-Only Drill

Check and recheck the grip following the basic fundamentals. This drill may be practiced indoors with a grip only. The purpose of the drill is to instill the importance of grip.

Full Swing: Five-Position Drill

I call this the *five-position drill* and usually use this drill with a large group. You want your students to demonstrate these five positions.

1. setup
2. backswing
3. top of the backswing
4. impact
5. follow-through

Call out the numbers of each position and have the children demonstrate each position. If you are unable to demonstrate these well yourself, use videos or photographs of golfers: children will mimic exactly what they see. Don't talk about mechanics; just show them the positions and then let them do each one. Here are some details to guide you.

1. Setup. This is the sound foundation that puts the golfer in the correct position to swing; it is the athletic or ready position. The feet are shoulder-width apart on the ground, with the weight distributed evenly between the right and left foot. Bend over from the hips, and tilt a little to the right/rear side with the upper body (reverse this for a left-hander).

The knees should be slightly flexed, and the arms should hang naturally. The golfer will remain in this posture throughout the swing.

2. **Backswing.** Move the club away using the left/target shoulder and arms and transfer the weight to the inside of the right/rear leg. The club is parallel to the ground when it is halfway back.

3. **Top of the backswing.** The weight is on the right/rear foot and the club is pointing over the right/rear shoulder to the target. The back is to the target.

4. **Impact.** The club returns to the position it was in at setup. Weight is on the left/target side, and the right/rear heel is off the ground.

5. **Follow-through.** Finish with the weight on the left/target leg, with the tummy and chest facing the target and the club over the left/target shoulder. The right/rear shoulder is now closer to the target than the left/target shoulder.

Remember, no mechanics. Just show the five positions, numbered 1 through 5. Call out each number and have the children demonstrate the static position.

Swing: Broom Drill

Set up with a lobby broom (see page 62)—the handle should reach about to the child's waist. Paste a different color piece of poster-board paper on either side of the head of the broom. You can also substitute a smiling face for the colored paper if you'd like, or paint the broom a different color on each side.

The broom I use has a red side and a green side. Demonstrate for the child the steps of this drill, explaining as you go: Set up with the broom as if you were addressing the ball, with the green side facing the target. Swing back and through a few times to get the feeling of a swing. Then swing to the top of the backswing; if the hands are in the correct position, only the green side should be visible. At impact, the green

Broom drill. Swinging with a short broom helps young golfers hold the follow-through.

side should be facing the target. In the finish position, only the red side should be visible. Now let the child go through the process. The purpose of this drill is to use the colors to put the hands into the correct position at the top, at impact, and in the follow-through (see photo, page 85). 🏌️①

Swing: Rhyme Drill

Set up with the broom and have the child repeat the following rhyme while swinging the broom, as described in the previous drill.

> *Swing back to the target,*
> *Thumbs to the sky.*
> *Belly to the target*
> *And the broom passes by.*

The purpose of the drill is to coordinate the backswing, forward swing, and the follow-through. 🏌️①

Setup: Railroad Track Drill

Place two clubs on the ground; they should be parallel to each other and pointing to the target (see top illustration page 49). Have your golfer visualize a railroad track and place the head of her club beside the outer track; her feet should be perpendicular to the inner track. Have her check her alignment and posture in a mirror. The purpose of this drill is to reinforce setup and alignment. 🏌️① → 🏌️③

Swing: Thumbs-Up Drill

Set up without a club. Place hands together as if they were gripping a club. Move the left/target shoulder, arms, and hands away from the target. Point the thumbs to the sky at waist height on the backswing. Point the thumbs to the sky at waist height on the follow-through. The purpose of this drill is to emphasize a one-piece takeaway—shoulder, arms, and hands, rather than just hands. 🏌️① → 🏌️③

Swing: Buckle Drill

Set up with or without a club. The golfer turns his back to the target on the backswing and turns his stomach or belt buckle to the target on the forward swing or downswing. The purpose of the drill is to feel that the arms are swinging naturally, and to feel the movements coordinated with little effort. Use verbal clues such as "turn and return," "swing back and through," or "swing 1 and 2" to help the golfer with tempo. 🏌️① → 🏌️③

Swing: Turn and Return Drill

Have your golfer set up in the correct posture, but without a club and with the arms crossed over the chest. Turn the left/target shoulder back level.

The right/rear shoulder goes up and behind and the upper body is coiled over the right/rear leg, which remains flexed. On the downswing, the weight moves to the left/target side and the shoulders rotate to the finish. The purpose of this drill is to eliminate the left/target shoulder dipping on the backswing (see photo, right). This is achieved when the golfer feels his shoulders turn away level on the backswing. Another tip for a level shoulder turn is to set up in the correct posture, and turn away with the left/target shoulder and get the feeling that you are looking over a banister at the top of the stairs; the upper body turns over the right/rear leg, which remains flexed. 🏌️ → 🏌️

Turn and Return Drill. The golfer on the right is using a ball between his knees to work on developing a stable base and a quiet lower body.

Swing: Beach Ball Drill #1

Set up, using a beach ball instead of a club (you can also use a basketball or medicine ball for older kids; use a weight appropriate for the child). Have the kids hold the ball in their hands and swing back and through and hold the finish. They swing back and through again, and stop at impact. They swing back and through again, but this time release the ball after impact. The purpose of the drill is for kids to get the feeling of using the lower body in the downswing (see photos, below). 🏌️ → 🏌️

Beach Ball Drill. Practicing the swing with a beach ball gives golfers the feeling of using the lower body in the downswing.

PITCHING AND FULL SWING

Swing: Beach Ball Drill #2

Set up with a beach ball, basketball, or light medicine ball (this drill is more effective with a slightly heavier ball, but use a weight appropriate for the child). He swings the ball back; at the top of the backswing, he releases the ball over the right/rear shoulder toward the target. The ball should travel left of the target when released correctly; if the child flicks his hands, the ball will end up right of the target (reverse for left-handers).The purpose of the drill is to create a full shoulder turn.

Swing: Toss Drill

Set up with the right/rear arm only (no club); the left/target hand is on the hip. She turns away with the left/target shoulder. The right/rear elbow folds, with the weight now on the right/rear side. Then she transfers the weight back to the left/target side, tosses underarm with the right/rear hand, and follows through. The purpose of this drill is to coordinate the upper and lower body. A tennis ball may be used for the drill. A right-hander sets up with the tennis ball in her right hand; a left-hander reverses this drill and sets up with the tennis ball in his left hand.

Swing: Baseball Drill

Have your golfer swing a baseball bat. She starts in the baseball position, and then she begins to lower the bat slightly with each swing. She remains in posture throughout the swing. Remind the golfer that she's standing up to a ball on the ground in a golf setup, just as in a batting position. This drill helps a young golfer avoid chopping at the ball and throwing the club head at the ball. This drill may also be used for older kids.

Swing: Tennis Racquet and Baseball Bat Drill

Stand or crouch down a few feet facing and well to the side away from your young golfer—do *not* position yourself to either side of the child (her target

Tennis Racquet and Baseball Bat Drill. This teaches swinging in balance.

or rear side). She sets up with a tennis racquet as for the golf swing. Lightly toss her a tennis ball and have her swing at and hit the ball and then follow through. Reinforce holding the follow-through. Once she does consistently well with the tennis racquet, allow her to progress to a baseball bat.

This drill is excellent for teaching swinging in balance; it's useful for kids of any age (see photo, left).

Swing: Paddle Drill

Use a table tennis paddle to demonstrate a square club face at impact (see photo, right). Paint one side of the paddle green and the other side red, painting little toes on the red side or pasting on toes cut from paper. The child grips the paddle and sets up as for the golf swing with the red side facing the target. At the top of the backswing, kids see the red side, with the toes pointing to the sky. In the follow-through, they see the green side.

Paddle Drill. Demonstrates the club face position and the swing.

Stable Base: Beach Ball Knee Drill

Set up without a club, with a beach ball between the knees (see photo page 87). The golfer turns the upper body over the right/rear leg, which remains flexed, then returns the upper body over the left/target leg. The purpose of this drill is to promote a stable base and a quiet lower body.

Firm Target Side: Towel Drill

The golfer sets up with a towel rather than a club in the left/target hand, right/rear hand on the hip. She swings the towel back and through so that the towel is flowing through to the finish. The purpose of the drill is to feel a firm left/target side through impact.

Impact: Whoosh Drill

Set up with a wood. The golfer inverts the club and grips the club just below the wooden head. He grips the club in the left/target hand; the right/rear hand is on the right/rear hip. He sets up with the club off the ground and swings the club back and through. Ask your golfer at what point he hears the *whoosh* sound. He should hear the *whoosh* at the point the club contacts the ball. The purpose of this drill is to increase acceleration through impact.

Impact Bag Drill. This drill helps re-create the feeling of impact.

Impact: Impact Bag Drill

Set up to an impact bag (see page 62) in the *impact position* (see page 79, photo #4). The impact position is like the setup position, except the hips are slightly open. The left/target arm, left/target wrist, and the back of the left/target hand are in a line with the club head. The right/rear heel has released off the ground, and the head remains behind the ball. The purpose of the drill is to re-create the feeling of impact using the impact bag (see photo, left). **①** → **③**

Relaxation: Tennis Ball Practice Drill

Place a tennis ball, a sponge ball, or a rubber ball on a tee. Rather than setting up to the ball, the child is two steps away. Holding the club off the ground, the child approaches the ball from the side in a right step (beginning the backswing) and then a left step (beginning the forward swing), and hits the ball. She will feel her weight transfer with the second step (left foot—reverse instructions for left-handers). This is a wonderful drill to teach relaxation and natural swing. Older kids can do this drill with golf balls. **①** → **③**

Pitching and Full-Swing Games
Pitching Games

Here are a handful of games you can use to practice pitching. These games can also be played indoors (in a garage or gym) with whiffle balls or sponge balls.

Through the Hoop Game

Set up three hoops and attach them to different uprights in the ground. Each hoop is at a different height. The goal is to pitch the ball through the hoop. Award points for successes.

Over the Bar Game

Tie a string between trees or uprights. Have the child pitch the ball over the string. Award points for successes.

Avoid the Swamp Game

Set up a tee box 25 to 50 yards from a target. Tell your young golfer there is an imaginary swamp between the tee and the target. There should be a large landing area, divided into three or four sections. Each section should be worth a certain number of points. The goal is to land the ball in the area worth the most points, or as close to that area as possible. The designated areas are worth 1, 2, 3, and 4 points. If the ball lands in the "swamp," there is a 2-point deduction.

Umbrella or Basket Game

The young golfer pitches the ball from varied distances into an open umbrella or a basket. Award 2 points for every ball holed and 1 point for every rimmed ball. A rimmed ball is one that hits the edge of the umbrella or basket and bounces out.

Full-Swing Games

Land the Ball in the Fairway Game

Set up on the driving range. Select an area about 50 yards wide to be the "fairway." The goal is to have your young golfer land all balls in the fairway. For every ball that lands in the fairway, the player earns 2 points. The ball does not have to be airborne: the goal is to hit the ball straight.

Target Game

The golfer stands 30 to 50 yards away from a target—a flag on a green 20 yards long and 10 to 15 yards wide. She hits balls to the target, earning 2 points for every ball that finishes at the target. The ball does not have to be airborne: the goal is to help the child become target oriented.

Golf Hole on the Range Game

Have the child play an imaginary par-3, -4, or -5 hole on the driving range, in the car, or in the house. If they're playing on the range, they use the club necessary for each particular shot. The child must visualize the hole, the shape of the hole, and the environment, such as trees, ducks, water, and shrubs. The child will tell you which club they used, where each ball landed, and the length of the putt. Never ask the score: ask instead how the shot felt. Kids love to play this game, and I for one would love to see Karrie Webb or Darren Clarke play holes designed by these imaginative course architects!

Open Space Game

Set up a golf hole in a large open space where the golfer can play the ball from a starting point to a finishing point. Count all the strokes. All attempts to strike the ball must be counted. Give kids the chance to set up a golf hole with water hazards and bunkers. Modify the game and use different size balls to suit the child's skill level. The ball size can also vary from anything from a beach ball to a golf ball. Be creative: use colored construction paper, plastic, strings, or talcum powder to set up the bunkers, water hazards, and the green.

Other Games to Teach Fundamentals

Charades

Write golf terms on index cards. With your young golfers, take turns picking a card from the "deck" and acting out the word on the card. This is a wonderful way to have fun and learn golf terminology at the same time.

Flash Cards Game

Write golf terms and rules on index cards. When a card is picked, have someone explain the term or the rule. This game can be played anywhere and helps kids learn terminology and rules.

Crossword Puzzle Game

Design crossword puzzles using golf terms. This is a good way for kids to focus on golf terms and concepts.

Rules Cloth Game

Place a large bedsheet or length of plain fabric on the ground or hang it on the wall. Kids use markers in different colors to draw a hole with teeing ground, the green, hazards (water and bunkers), trees, and the cart path. Award kids 1 point for reciting a rule associated with a certain area. Point to an area and ask them to explain a penalty associated with that area.

Questions and Answers

Q. I have had three lessons with my son. And while he is really enjoying himself, he just isn't getting the skills. I have been trying to build on what I have done, but I feel as if I have to keep repeating the basics.

A. Your son is only a child, and you will have to repeat and reteach those basic skills every day. Once your son is having fun and showing an interest, you are on the road to building a golf swing. He may need ten to twenty lessons before grasping the basics enough to take them to the course. Golf is a lifetime sport, but it's a very difficult game that takes years to master. Be patient.

Q. My daughter has mastered all the drills and minigames in the book. What should I do next?

A. Drills are never mastered! Together you need to set higher goals for her: is she putting and chipping every ball into the hole? Both of you can use your imaginations to improvise. Make the drills gamelike and more competitive. Look for a higher standard for every drill, especially on drills that work on grip, posture, alignment, and the stroke.

Q. My son only wants to hit his woods every day. Is it OK to let him hit the woods occasionally instead of giving him an organized lesson?

A. Yes! It *is* good to give kids a break from routine. He will enjoy the short game skills more at the next lesson.

Q. My daughter always whines when I invite her for a lesson. Then, when we have the lesson, she enjoys it. What should I do?

A. Golf is fun and recreational. If your daughter is not interested, she should not be forced to play. Wait for her to ask you to play or to ask you for a lesson.

CHAPTER 7

Bunker Shots

Kids love the bunker. They have so much fun, it's almost as good as a day at the beach. But most adult golfers don't share their enthusiasm, and the sand shot is the most feared shot in golf. But it's also the easiest shot: the sand shot is the only shot where you don't have to hit the ball with the club! In fact, in the explosion shot, the force with which you hit the sand adjacent to the ball drives the ball—so the club face never comes in direct contact with the ball.

Most amateur golfers fear this shot for a number of reasons, the principle reason being that they seldom get to practice it. They may not find themselves in a bunker during an entire round, so when they eventually find their ball in the sand, they are intimidated.

Basics
Work from Confidence

Children don't show fear in the sand unless you have instilled it in them. In your teaching, approach the sand shot as you would any other shot. There is nothing complicated about the basic sand shot, so keep the instructions very simple at the beginning. The main objective from the sand is to get the ball out. When your golfer has mastered that with consistency, she can then make adjustments to get the ball close to the hole. If your child practices the sound fundamentals of the sand shot, she'll approach the bunker with confidence and make the sand her friend.

Which Club?

The club to use from the sand is the sand wedge. The sand wedge is built for getting the ball out of the sand: it has more loft, a bigger flange compared with other irons, and it's also heavier. With this in mind, allow the club to do the work. The more complicated you make it for a child, the less successful she will be. (If the child doesn't have a sand wedge, she can use a pitching wedge.)

Explosion Shot

An *explosion shot* is a shot made from the sand a short distance from the green. Allow your golfer to use the swing she learned for the pitch shot, but with a few adjustments. Hitting close to the green, the player swings with the intent of taking sand from the bunker. The ball should come out of the sand and the club face does not touch the ball.

She gets into the practice bunker and digs her feet into the sand. Draw two parallel lines in the sand about 4 inches apart (remind the golfer this is allowed only in the practice bunker) and perpendicular to the target: the back line is in the center of the stance; the front line is off the left/target heel. She sets up in a slightly open stance, with the left/target foot back a little, and squares the club face to the back (rear) line—see photo, below. With her eyes on the back (rear) line, she makes a swing, sweeping both lines out of the sand with the club face (the resulting spray of sand is the "explosion"). She then makes ten similar swings, with the objective of sweeping *both* lines out of the sand with the swing (if she sweeps only one of the lines in practice, when she is swinging with the ball in place, the club will strike the ball directly, and it will fly too far). If your golfer is successful, have her try the process with a ball between the lines. She sets the club face up to the back (rear) line (in the center of the stance). Keeping her eyes on the back line rather than on the ball, she makes her pitch swing and follow-through. In a successful sand shot, the club face never touches the ball; the ball comes out on a rectangular piece of sand. Remind the golfer that, in a game, touching the sand at address or with a practice swing will incur a penalty.

These are the steps to follow to guide children through the basic sand shot.

1. Set up slightly open (as you would for the pitch shot).
2. Set your weight on the left/target side.
3. Dig the feet into the sand.
4. Draw two parallel lines in the sand: one in the center of the stance and one off the left/target heel (this is allowed only in the practice bunker).

Although you can't do this in standard play, drawing two lines in the sand of the bunker (about 4 inches apart) will give you feedback from your swing.

The sand bunker shot is the only shot in golf where success comes when you *don't* hit the ball. Hit the sand behind the ball and follow through. Grounding the club in the sand is not permitted.

5. Place a ball between the two lines.

6. With eyes on the back (rear) line, swing the club back to L-shape at waist height.

7. Keep the weight on the left/target side; the head remains steady.

8. Swing through the back (rear) line and follow through the front (target) line and finish high. Keep the left/target arm moving through to the finish.

9. The weight finishes on the left/target side.

The keys to a successful sand shot are a slow, smooth takeaway; an L-shaped backswing, formed by the arms and the club at waist height; watching the sand behind the ball; and the follow-through. Longer shots require more club head speed and a higher finish. Remind your golfer to keep the left/target arm moving through to the finish. Practice builds confidence.

Beyond the Basic Sand Shot

As soon as your child shows lots of confidence with the explosion shot and sets a goal of getting closer to the hole, one more adjustment may be added. Have him open the club face (see illustration page 80; the club face is open if it's aiming to the right of the target for a right-hander; reverse this for a left-hander). Do this before he grips the club. He will now be set up to the target with an open stance and an open club face. I do not recommend an open club face unless your young golfer is very advanced. Until he reaches that point, he will get excellent results with a square club face. Remember, keep the instructions simple in the beginning.

Longer and Shorter Shots from the Greenside Bunker

The only adjustment required for a longer shot is to increase the club head speed and follow-through higher—the club still doesn't touch the ball. For a shorter shot, finish lower. Do not shorten the backswing: it should remain constant.

Buried Lie

A golfer uses a different technique when the ball is buried in the sand than when it's lying on the sand. Have her set up square, with the ball in the center of the stance. Her weight should be to the left/target side. She grips the club normally, then turns the toe of the club inward. This will help dig the ball out of the sand. She makes a shorter backswing and swings into the sand about 2 inches behind the ball, then finishes the swing at the ball. The ball will come out low and roll more.

Uphill Bunker Shot

For an uphill bunker shot, the golfer must adjust his address position and set up with a slightly open stance. He should set his shoulders parallel to the slope of the bunker; in other words, the angle of his shoulders should match the angle of the slope. His weight will be on the right/rear/downhill foot. He will then square up the club face and play the ball off his left/target heel. He should swing along the slope and finish high.

Downhill Bunker Shot

The downhill bunker shot is the most difficult bunker shot. Again, the golfer should adjust her address position to the shape of the slope. The weight will be on the left/target/downhill side, with the ball near the right/rear foot. As with the uphill shot, the angle of her shoulders matches the angle of the slope. She swings the club upward on the backswing, then swings down the slope. She follows through low.

Fairway Bunker Shot

This is the only bunker shot where the golfer actually wants to hit the ball. The club to use in a fairway bunker shot is very dependent on the lie in the bunker. For the beginner, I would recommend playing a midiron, provided there is no lip on the bunker. A midiron is a 6- or 5-iron, which kids with a limited set of clubs might not have. If this is the case, they can use a 7-iron if that is the least-lofted club in their bag. From a fairway bunker, he would *not* use the sand wedge, since he's a longer distance from the green.

He plays the shot like an ordinary iron shot. He sets up with the weight evenly distributed and plays the ball back in the stance. He grips down the club shaft and addresses the ball with the hands ahead of the ball. He keeps the body steady throughout the swing and aims at the top half of the ball in order to hit it cleanly.

Drills for the Bunker

Practice builds confidence. You can help a child build confidence in the sand with drills that are done both with and without a ball. These are drills you'll use in the practice bunker. But on the course, remind the child that when he addresses a ball lying in a bunker, he'll incur a two-stroke penalty if he lets the club head touch the sand at address.

Tempo: Closed Eyes Drill

The golfer makes swings in the sand with the eyes closed. She feels the club swing through the sand. The purpose of the drill is to develop a slow, smooth swing. 🔴 → 🔴

Taking Sand: Line Drill

Place two parallel lines in the sand 4 inches apart (see photo page 95). Set up with the lines extending from the toes, with the back line in the center of the stance and the front line just to the inside of the target foot. The golfer sets the club up to the back line. He makes swings taking both lines out of the sand. He keeps the lower body steady, and the weight on the left/target side. Always follow through. The purpose of the drill is to take sand and not the ball; in a proper shot, the ball will come out with the sand. The lines help the player move enough sand so that the ball pops out on the sand. 🔴 → 🔴

Taking Sand: Dollar Bill Drill

Draw a rectangle in the sand about 2½ by 6 inches—the size of a dollar bill. Set up perpendicular to the dollar bill to swing; the club face sweeps both the back (rear) and front (target) lines out of the dollar bill. She places a ball in the center of the imaginary dollar bill and sets the leading edge of the club to the back line of the dollar bill. She swings the club, entering the sand on the back (rear) line and exiting the sand on the front (target) line, and out pops the ball. Follow-through is high. The purpose of this drill is to take a dollar's worth of sand from the bunker! 🔴 → 🔴

Swing: Tee Drill

Place the ball on a tee in the sand. The tee should be low enough so the ball is level with the sand. The golfer swings in order to knock the tee from under the ball, and follows through. The ball will fly onto the green. The purpose of the drill is to make the player enter the sand behind the ball and to follow through. 🔴 → 🔴

Distance: Alternate Splash Drill

Draw parallel lines in the sand, just as we did in the Line Drill, above. The lines extend from the toes, with the back (rear) line in the center of the stance and the front (target) line just to the inside of the left/target foot. The golfer alternates short, medium, and long swings. He swings through the lines: a short swing will cause the sand to land close to the edge of the green; a longer swing will put the sand farther in on the green. Observe together where the sand lands on the green. Remember, this is the only shot where the golfer never hits the ball: the ball will come out atop the sand. Now he places a ball in the sand and plays short, medium, and long shots. The purpose of the drill is to relate club head speed and finish to distance. The shorter the swing, the shorter the distance the sand travels and the shorter the distance the ball will travel. ① → ③

CHAPTER 8

Special Shots

The great Seve Ballesteros has stated often that he uses his instinct and imagination to play golf. This has to be the reason for his wizardry around the green and his mastery of those challenging shots. As a teacher and golfer, I have such great admiration for Seve Ballesteros for a number of reasons, among them that he came from humble beginnings and wasn't a member of a golf club or country club. Even without the opportunities of his peers, he was determined to become the maestro that he is today—even if he had to play the game for many years with only one club. Because of this, he learned to play every shot in the book through visualization and imagination. Of course, he also had some other ingredients that are needed for success: a love for the game, a hunger to practice, a desire within, and talent.

The exciting thing about golf is that the "playing field" changes with every shot. Some golf courses are flat; others are hilly. Golfers also have to play around trees and make adjustments for wind. Making these special shots is all part of the challenge. The secret is to visualize the ball flight and learn to shape the shot—by shaping the shot, they will try to make it fly from right to left or from left to right. They may wish to hit the ball high or low. Children must have a good foundation with the basics in order to teach themselves to play special shots, most of which are for the advanced junior. What a great opportunity for children to use their imagination, see the shot in their minds, and use their bodies to shape the shot.

Hilly Lies

The most common situation on a hilly course is understanding how to deal with *uphill*, *downhill*, and *sidehill* lies. In the following pages, you'll learn how to coach your child in making adjustments from her normal setup and swing in these situations.

Allow kids to experiment with these shots on the practice tee. Kids love to play the game over, under, and around real or imagined obstacles.

Ask them how they did and how they played various shots. Practice will build confidence—and more practice will build even more confidence.

Uphill Lie

The *uphill lie*, when the ball is on an upward slope, is the easiest of the uneven lies to play. A golfer needs to make the following adjustments to her regular setup. She should use a less lofted club than she would normally play on a flat lie. For example, if her ball landed on a flat surface and the next shot would call for an 8-iron, she would use a 7-iron for the same distance on an uphill lie. Have the child grip down the shaft and play the ball forward in the stance, off the left/target foot. Her weight in the stance, which should be narrow, will favor the right/downhill foot. As we did on an uphill bunker shot, the angle of the shoulders should match the angle of the slope. Using a compact swing, have her swing along the angle of the slope and follow through. An uphill shot has a tendency to go to the left because of the slope, so aim to the right of the target (reverse for the left-hander).

This golfer demonstrates the correct setup for an *uphill lie.*

Downhill Lie

The *downhill lie*, when the ball is on a down slope, is the most difficult of the uneven lies to play because the tendency is to follow through high instead of swinging down the slope. The following adjustments must be made to the regular setup. Use one club less. For example, if the distance on the flat would normally call for a 7-iron, use an 8-iron for the same distance from a downhill lie. Widen the stance and put the weight on the left/target/front foot, which is the downhill foot, and play the ball toward the right/rear foot. The swing is compact and should match the

Have your child study this golfer's proper setup for a *downhill lie.*

angle of the slope. A downhill shot has a tendency to go to the right because of the slope, so aim to the left of the target (reverse for the left-hander). Follow through down the slope.

Sidehill Lie

There are two types of sidehill lies. A golfer can play the ball from above his feet, or he can play the ball from below his feet.

- **Playing the ball above the feet.** This shot calls for some adjustments to a normal setup. The player grips down the shaft and plays one club less than he would normally play on a flat lie. For example, he would choose a 7-iron instead of a 6-iron. He plays the ball from the center of a narrow stance. He flexes the knees and leans into the hill, toward the toes. Aim farther up the hill with the body and club face to compensate slightly for the slope and the ball's natural tendency to move downhill. For example, a right-hander will aim right since the ball has a tendency to fall to the left. A left-hander will aim left since the ball would fall to the right. Shorten the backswing and swing in balance, maintaining balance and posture throughout the swing.

- **Playing the ball below the feet.** A sidehill shot with the ball below the feet is very difficult. Instruct your young golfer to make the following adjustments. He moves his grip toward the top of the shaft and uses one club more than he would normally from a flat lie; that is, use a 7-iron instead of an 8-iron. He bends at the hips, widens the stance, and plays the ball from the center of the stance. Leaning into the hill—in this case toward the heels—he aims the ball uphill, as it will have a tendency to fall downhill. A right-hander would aim left; a left-hander would aim right. He swings within himself (that is, he doesn't swing too hard) and maintains his balance throughout the swing.

This golfer has made the proper adjustments for playing the ball below his feet on a *sidehill lie*.

Tips for Hilly Lies

Review these tips for playing hilly lies with your young golfing buddy.

- swing with the slope
- swing in balance and retain your posture

- use one club less for the ball you play above the feet or on a down-hill lie
- use one club more for the ball you play below the feet or an uphill lie

Around Trees

The playing field for golf can be affected by the placement of trees, and golfers must be able to make the appropriate adjustments. But don't worry: kids love the challenge of playing shots from behind or under trees. Here are some of the situations a golfer will face.

Punch Shot: Playing from Under a Tree

If you are under a tree and unsure of the type of shot to play, chip out to the side and play it safe. But if the branches are hanging low and there is a clear path to the green, a low running shot—a shot that has a lower trajectory, to avoid hanging branches—may be the answer. Instruct your golfer to make the following adjustments for the punch shot.

Use a club with less loft, which will keep the ball low. For example, choose a 5- or 6-iron if the shot without the trees would call for a 7-iron. Grip down on the shaft and place the hands ahead of the ball at the address. Play the ball in the back of a square stance, with the weight favoring the left/target foot. Swing within yourself, with the hands leading, and follow through low.

Again, using a club with less loft will keep the ball low and help avoid low-hanging branches. Any club below a 7-iron is the appropriate club for this shot.

Playing from Behind a Tree

Here, the golfer has to look at the situation and decide if the best choice is to play over the tree, around the tree, or chip out to the side. The most sensible option from behind a tree may be to play it safe and chip to the side. But read on for other options.

High Shot

A high shot over the tree may be the choice, if the club has enough loft to clear the tree. The golfer makes the following adjustments for this shot. She sets up with the ball forward in the stance and squares the club face. She places the hands even with, or a little behind, the ball. She keeps the head behind the ball throughout the swing, and finishes with a high follow-through.

Playing around a Tree

The ball may be close to a tree, and your golfer will have the option of playing the ball around the tree. Here, a golfer has several options.

If the path is clear to the green on the right side of the tree, have the child set up to play the ball with a right-to-left ball flight. This is called a *draw* or a *hook*. A draw is when the ball curves a little from right to left, and a hook is when the ball curves a lot from right to left.

When the only clear pathway is on the left side of the tree, set up to play the ball with a left-to-right ball flight. This is called a *fade* or a *slice*. A fade is when the ball curves a little from left to right, and a slice is when the ball curves a lot from left to right. Read on for instructions on how to help your golfer with these special shots.

- **Draw or hook.** Set the feet and body on the line on which you intend to start the ball around the tree. Use a slightly closed stance and set the club face directly at the target. The ball will draw from right to left. Have your child swing on an in-to-out swing path, using a light grip. The club travels from inside the target line on the downswing, to square at impact, to outside the target line in the follow-through.

  A stronger grip may also be appropriate. Here, the golfer will see more than two knuckles on the target hand. Make minor adjustments for a draw and greater adjustments for a hook. The draw flies lower and rolls more than a fade (see below).

- **Fade or slice.** Set the feet and body on the line on which you intend to start the ball around the tree, using a slightly open stance. Grip the club firmly and set the club face directly at the target; then swing on an out-to-in swing path. The ball will fade from left to right. An out-to-in swing is when the club travels from outside the target line on the downswing, to square at the impact, to inside the target line at the follow-through.

  A weaker grip may also be appropriate. Here, the golfer will only see one knuckle on the left/target hand. The weaker grip will open the club face and, combined with an out-to-in swing path, will cause a slice. Make minor adjustments for a fade and major adjustments for a slice. The fade flies higher and rolls less than a draw.

Encourage children to experiment with different shots and different situations. They should learn to curve the ball intentionally. Plus, they'll have fun learning what causes the ball to draw and fade.

Wind

When the wind blows on the golf course, golf can become a totally different game. The biggest mistake that golfers make in the wind is to swing too hard and too fast. A strong headwind or tail wind may call for a club choice that is two to three clubs more (or less) than normal. Playing in the wind requires an understanding of the fundamental adjustments and a wonderful tempo.

Headwind: Playing into the Wind

In a headwind, with the wind in the golfer's face, instruct your child to make the following adjustments. Grip down the shaft for control and use more club than normal, depending on the strength of the wind. For example, choose a 5- or 6-iron instead of a 7-iron. Play the ball back in a square stance. The stance should be wider than normal for control. If you're playing from the tee, tee the ball a little lower than you would for a normal shot, since you want to keep the ball low into the wind. Swing under control, using normal tempo.

When the wind is behind your back, teeing the ball higher will usually add distance to your shot. With the wind in your face, teeing the ball a little lower will keep the ball from gaining height and losing distance.

Tail Wind: Playing with the Wind from Behind

When the wind is blowing from behind the golfer, make these adjustments. Grip down the shaft and use one club less than normal, depending on the wind. For example, choose a 5-iron instead of a 4-iron. Play from a square stance with the ball forward in the stance. Make a normal swing with a high follow-through. Use good tempo and tee the ball high, if you're playing from the teeing ground. The ball forward in the stance and teed higher will promote higher trajectory and help the ball travel farther in the wind.

Crosswind

Playing in a crosswind can play havoc with your score. The simplest way to play a shot in these conditions is to let the wind blow the ball back to the target. Instruct your golfer to play the ball into the wind and then allow the wind to carry the ball to the target. Swing within yourself—swing in control using normal tempo.

- **Left-to-right wind.** When the wind is blowing from left to right, set up to the left of the target and let the wind carry the ball back to the target.

wind blowing from the left, aim left

wind blowing from the right, aim right

When hitting into a left or right crosswind, adjust your aim and let the wind carry the ball to the target.

teeing ground

- **Right-to-left wind.** When the wind is blowing from right to left, set up to the right of the target, and let the wind carry the ball back to the target.

Drills for Special Shots

Finding an area to practice special shots may be difficult. It is not always possible to practice uphill, downhill, and sidehill lies at the golf course. Use golf whiffle balls to practice uneven lies and practice on the side of an elevated teeing ground or on a hilly fairway; this way, the ball will not travel far. Always secure permission from the club manager, the course superintendent, or the golf pro if you wish to practice these shots on the golf course or at the side of an elevated teeing ground.

Adjustment for Hilly Lies

Set up on the side of a hill and make the appropriate adjustments for each type of lie. Always use golf whiffle balls. The goal of the drill is for your young golfers to become familiar with the adjustments needed for each type of lie. They will need to make these adjustments automatically if they are confronted with a hilly lie on the golf course. Remind them to observe the ball flight from each lie.

Fade or Draw Drill

Set up on the driving range and visualize a tree directly in front of you. Make the adjustments necessary to play the ball around the tree and to a target directly behind the tree. Have the child learn to shape the ball to the right of the tree and then to the left of the tree. The goal is to practice hitting the ball with left-to-right and right-to-left ball flights.

High and Low Trajectory Drill

To help your golfer play a high ball, set up at the driving range and visualize a tree 20 yards in front. Have him make the necessary adjustments to play the ball over the tree. To play a low ball from under tree branches, he visualizes the ball directly under low-hanging branches. Have him make the necessary adjustments to play the ball low.

APPENDIX: The Rules Simplified

The rules of golf are there to help you, not hinder you. Understanding the rules can be to your advantage. Adults should familiarize themselves with the rules and always carry an official rules book in their bag.

All the rules are of equal importance. But some situations will arise on a daily basis, and these should be covered and explained repeatedly to children. Children should know the penalty incurred and the procedure to follow. Remember, children are their own rules officials in tournaments: they must call the penalties on themselves, and they can only do this correctly if they understand the basic rules.

- The player must count all strokes; even a whiff counts.
- The ball is hit from the teeing ground. It must be played from between the markers or within two club lengths behind the markers. There is a two-stroke penalty for an infringement of the rule, and the ball must be replayed. When addressing the ball on the teeing ground, there is no penalty if the ball moves, for the ball is not yet in play.
- The player who had the best score on the previous hole receives the honor.
- If the ball moves at address anywhere on the course, except on the teeing ground, it is a one-stroke penalty and the ball must be replaced to the original position.
- If the player does not address the ball and it moves, there is no penalty; you can play the ball as it lies.
- If the ball is lost or out of bounds, a penalty stroke must be added and the ball must be played from the original position.
- A provisional ball may be played if you are unsure whether your ball is lost or out of bounds. If you find the original ball, it is the ball in play.
- A player is allowed five minutes to search for the ball; you must always call the group behind through.
- If a ball lands on a cart path, in casual water, or in ground under repair, proceed under the rules and drop the ball without penalty.
- Drop the ball by standing erect, hold the ball at shoulder height and arm's length, and then drop.
- If the ball lands in a bunker or hazard, you may not ground the club while addressing the ball. If the club is grounded, you incur a two-stroke penalty.
- A ball may be played from a water hazard without penalty, or you may drop out of the hazard under a penalty of one stroke.
- Loose impediments—such as twigs, unattached branches, leaves—may be removed anywhere on the course except in a hazard. If the ball moves while removing a loose impediment within one club length of the ball, you incur a one-stroke penalty and the ball must be replaced.

- While on the putting green, always ask your playing partner to mark their ball; it is a two-stroke penalty if your ball hits the other player's ball or the flag while on the green. Play your ball as it lies and replace the other ball.
- Always replace the flag, and record the score at the next teeing ground.
- Both players sign and date the scorecard after the round.

Glossary

You and your young golfing buddy should familiarize yourself with these important golf terms. See drills and games in chapter 5 (beginning on page 59) and chapter 6 (beginning on page 83) to help children remember them.

Ace: See *hole in one*.

Address the ball: Taking your stance and grounding the club (except in a hazard) before you swing. When a player is in a hazard, she has addressed the ball when she has taken her stance.

All square: The term used in match play to indicate that the match is level or even.

Approach: Any shot played to the putting green, whether or not it lands there; also called *approach shot*.

Apron: The closely mowed area surrounding the putting green; also called the *fringe* or *collar*.

Away: The ball farthest from the hole, which is played before balls closer to the hole.

Back 9: The last 9 holes of an 18-hole course; is also called the *In nine* (from "In" on the scorecard).

Ball mark: Also called a *pitch mark*. The mark made to the green after an approach shot. The mark should be repaired with a pitch repair tool (or a tee) and then tapped down with the head of the putter.

Ball marker: A small coin-like object placed behind the ball before removing the ball from the putting green. A player may lift the ball and clean it while on the putting green.

Birdie: One stroke below par for a hole.

Bogey: One stroke over par for a hole.

Break: The tendency for the ball to roll down a slope on the green. For example, a putt may break to the right or the left, depending on the slope on the green.

Breaking putt: A putt that curves to the right or left of a hole on a sloping green.

Bunker: A hazard covered with sand. Often referred to incorrectly as a *trap* or *sand trap*.

Caddie: The person who carries the player's clubs. A player may receive advice from the caddie.

Carry: The distance that the ball is in the air from the time it leaves the club until it hits the ground.

Cart path: Path for golf carts; observe the cart rules.

Casual water: A temporary accumulation of water caused by rain or a sprinkler. A player may remove the ball from casual water without a penalty. A player gets relief if the ball or stance is affected by casual water.

Championship teeing ground: The teeing ground farthest from the green.

Chip: A shot made from just off the green; this is also known as a *pitch and run*. This shot has a very low trajectory.

Closed: The position of the feet on the ground. The right/rear foot is pulled back off the target line. The club face may also be closed if the leading edge is facing to the left of the target.

Club head: The club head has five components: the toe, heel, sole, face, and leading edge.

Course rating: The rating of the difficulty of the course. The rating system is determined by the USGA. It is based on the difficulty of each course and gives a quick computer adjustment (up or down) on the handicap. The result is that the player's handicap index becomes portable and it states how many strokes will be given at another course.

Cup: See *hole*.

Divot: The turf removed by a club while swinging. The divot should always be replaced.

Dogleg: A fairway with a sharp turn. A fairway that angles to the right is a *dogleg right*; the fairway that angles to the left is a *dogleg left*.

Dormie: A player or a side in match play is *dormie* when that player or side is as many holes ahead as the number of holes left to play. For example, "three holes ahead with three holes left to play."

Double bogey: Two strokes over par for a given hole.

Down: In match play, the number of holes a player or team is behind.

Draw: A shot that curves slightly from right to left (reverse for the left-hander). This shot results in more roll when it lands.

Driver: This club has the longest shaft and is the least-lofted club in the set. This club is usually used from the tee box and should propel the ball the longest distance.

Eagle: A score of two strokes under par for a given hole.

Error detection: Using ball flight, club path, and club face as feedback.

Executive course: A course slightly shorter than a regulation golf course. It has some par-4 holes, but most holes are par 3. This type of course is excellent for children and beginners.

Explosion shot: A shot from the sand.

Face: The area of the club head that strikes the ball.

Fade: A shot that curves slightly from left to right (reverse this for the left-hander). This shot results in less roll when it lands.

Fairway: The closely mowed area between the *teeing ground* and the *green*.

Fat: A fat shot is caused by hitting the ground behind the ball before striking the ball. This results in a weak shot with little distance.

Flagstick: This shows the location of the hole on the green. Incorrectly referred to as the *pin*.

Fore: A warning cry used on golf courses everywhere. When golfers hear this call, they turn away from the direction of the call and duck.

Forward teeing ground: See *teeing ground*.

Forward tees: See *tee markers*.

Fourball: A match in which two golfers play their better ball against the better ball of two other golfers, or in stroke play against the field.

Foursome: The most common grouping of players used to speed up play. Two players may often be grouped with two other players.

Fresh air: A miss when attempting to hit the ball. This counts as a stroke in official competition. This is also called a *whiff*.

Fringe: The name for the shorter grass around the green; also known as the *apron* or *collar*.

Front 9: The first 9 holes of an 18-hole course; also called the *Out nine* (from "Out" on the scorecard).

Full swing: The sequence of backswing, forward swing, and follow-through allowing the golfer to hit the ball a long distance.

Gimmie: In friendly play, a putt very close to the hole is conceded by the opponent. You do not have to putt, but you must count it as a stroke. In match play, the opponent may concede a putt.

Green: The putting surface.

Gross score: The total number of strokes for the round.

Grounding the club: Placing the sole or the flange of the club on the ground behind the ball.

Ground under repair: The white lined area on the golf course that is temporarily unfit for play. The ball may be lifted, cleaned, and dropped at the nearest point of relief away from the ground under repair.

Handicap: A method used to equalize the different abilities of players, resulting in each player having an individualized and updatable *handicap index*, which can be applied to any course with a USGA course rating to determine the player's course handicap. The approximate number of strokes a player shoots over par is allowed to equalize the player's ability.

Handicap index: A system of rating the difficulty factor of specific holes on a course. The hole rated as number 1 under the Handicap or Index column on the scorecard is the most difficult hole on the course; the hole rated as number 18 is the easiest hole on the course.

Halved: In a match play competition, the match is *halved* if both players won the same number of holes on an 18-hole course.

Hazard: Bunkers and water hazards (including lateral water hazards) on the course. The player may not ground the club in a hazard.

Hole: The 4¼-inch hole in the ground on the putting green; also called *cup*. Also, the complete area from tee to green; thus, "18 holes."

Hole in one: When a player hits the ball from the teeing ground into the hole in one stroke; this is also called an *ace*.

Hole out: To complete the play of a hole by putting or hitting the ball into the hole.

Honor: The player scoring the lowest score on the preceding hole gets the *honor*, which is the right to tee off first. On the first hole, the honor may be decided by the toss of a coin. Sometimes incorrectly referred to as *honors*.

Hook: A shot that curves drastically from right to left (reverse for the left-hander). Compare *slice*.

Hosel: The part of the club where the shaft and the head connect.

In-bounds area: Area in which play is allowed.

Iron: Irons are numbered from 3 to 9. They are categorized as long irons, midirons, and short irons.

Kick: The bounce of the ball after landing; or the flex in the shaft.

Lag putt: A long putt that stops close to the hole.

Lateral water hazard: Lake, pond, river, sea, or ditch that runs parallel to the line of the hole (a straight line from teeing ground to flagstick, accommodating doglegs). This area is marked with red stakes or red lines.

Lie: The position of the ball on the ground, or the lie of the club head on the ground. See also *winter rules*.

Lip: The edge of the hole or cup. Some missed putts are putts that have *lipped out*—the ball ran along the lip and then veered away from the hole.

Loft: The angle on the face of the club. The driver has the least loft and the sand wedge has the most loft.

Loose impediment: Objects such as twigs, branches (not growing), or leaves. Sand and soil are also considered loose impediments on the green, but not elsewhere. Loose impediments may not be removed from a hazard.

LPGA: Ladies Professional Golf Association, which encompasses both the playing and teaching divisions.

Marker: The individual in a competition who keeps the score.

Match play: In this type of competition, each hole is a separate contest. The winner is the player or team who wins the most number of holes. Compare *stroke play*.

Medal play: See *stroke play*.

Moved: A ball is deemed to have *moved* if it leaves the original position and comes to rest in another place.

Nassau: This is a type of friendly competition where one point is awarded for each nine holes and an additional point is awarded for the match. A total of three points are possible.

Net score: The number that results when a player's handicap is deducted from his gross score.

Open: The position of the feet or the club head in relation to the target line. The stance is open if the feet are aimed to the left of the target (for a left-hander, feet are aimed right of the target). The club face is open if it is aiming to the right of the target (to the left for a left-hander).

Open tournament: The type of competition in which both professionals and amateurs may participate. There is usually a qualifying round.

Out-of-bounds: Ground outside the boundaries of the golf course on which play is prohibited. Out-of-bounds areas are marked by white stakes.

Par: The standard of scoring excellence for each hole. This is expressed as a par 3, par 4, or a par 5 and is determined by the length of the hole.

Penalty stroke: A penalty stroke is added to the score of a player (or a side) for infringement of a rule.

PGA: Professional Golfers' Association. The association has both male and female members who are club professionals.

PGA Tour: An association of male players who play on regular tour events.

Pitch: A shot executed with a lofted club that produces a high trajectory and little roll.

Pitch and run: A shot with a very low trajectory played from just off the green. Also referred to as a *chip*.

Pitching wedge: A short iron with 48 degrees of loft. Used to play a high shot to the green.

Pitch mark: A mark left on the green from the high approach shot. These marks should be repaired. This is legal to do even if the mark is on the line of the putt.

Play through: Stepping aside and allowing the players behind you to move ahead. Helps avoid slow play.

Point of relief: The point at which relief may be taken. The nearest point of relief is the point on the course nearest to where the ball lies that is no closer to the hole and where no interference, as defined by the rules, exists.

Provisional ball: A ball played to substitute for a ball that may be lost (not lost in a hazard) or may be out-of-bounds. The provisional ball is used to speed up play. If the original ball is found, it must be played provided it was in bounds. Otherwise, the provisional ball is the ball in play.

Pull: A ball that flies on a straight path to the left of the target line (reverse for a left-hander).

Push: A ball that flies in a straight path to the right of the target line (reverse for a left-hander).

Putter: The club used on the putting green to put the ball in the hole.

R&A: Royal and Ancient Golf Club of St. Andrews, Scotland. The R&A and the United States Golf Association are the governing bodies of golf. They review and revise the rules of golf every two years.

Regular tees: See *tee markers*.

Relief: The options for moving a ball, according to the rules. See also *point of relief*.

Rough: The area bordering the fairway where the grass has been allowed to grow long.

Rub of the green: When a ball in motion or at rest is stopped or deflected by an outside agency.

Running shot: A shot with little air time and a lot of roll.

Sand trap: See *bunker*.

Sand wedge: The club used for playing shots from sand bunkers.

Scramble: A competition in which the entire team plays each shot from the ball in the best position. They all drop where the best ball lies.

Scratch player: A player who regularly scores close to par.

Scotch foursome: Two players playing as a team, using one ball and playing alternate shots.

Shaft: The part of the club that extends from the club head to the grip. This can be made of steel, graphite, boron, or other materials.

Shank: A shot where the ball is hit from the hosel of the club instead of the club face. The ball flies directly to the right (to the left for a left-hander).

Shape the shot: Intentionally hitting the ball right to left, left to right, or high or low.

Short-distance golf ball: Travels half the distance of the regular golf ball. Also known as a Cayman ball.

Slice: A shot that travels drastically from left to right (reverse for the left-hander). Compare *hook*.

Socket: See *shank*.

Sole: The part of the club that rests on the ground.

Square stance: To align the feet, knees, hips, and shoulders parallel to the target line, as if a railroad track.

Square the club: To align the club's leading edge perpendicular to the target line.

Stance: The position of the feet on the ground while addressing the ball.

Starter: The person employed by the golf course to send everyone off the first tee in an orderly and timely fashion. All players must report to the starter.

Stroke: The forward motion a player makes with the club with the intention of striking the ball. Each forward motion made with the intention of hitting the ball is a stroke and must be added to the score (i.e., whiffs count).

Stroke play: A competition in which all strokes are counted for the round. Compare *match play*.

Sweet spot: The area on the face of the club that strikes the ball perfectly. The professionals only hit approximately seven perfect shots per round.

Swing path: The path the club head travels from the top of the backswing through impact.

Takeaway: The beginning of the backswing.

Target: The spot where the ball should land.

Target line: The direct path between the ball and the target.

Tee: The tee is a wooden or plastic peg that is placed under the ball on the teeing ground. The verb *tee off* refers to planting the tee in the ground and hitting the first ball from a hole's *teeing ground*.

Teeing ground: The starting area for the hole being played. The teeing ground is a rectangle bordered in the front by a set (pair) of tee markers, and extending two club lengths in depth. The ball must be played between a set of markers or no more than two club lengths behind the markers. The player may stand outside the teeing ground, but the ball must be inside the defined area.

Tee markers: A set (pair) of markers on the teeing ground, each set a defined distance from the flagstick. The championship tees are farthest from the flagstick and are played by professional and scratch golfers. Forward tees are generally played by juniors, women, and seniors. The regular tees (middle) are used by all other players.

Tee time: The time at which your group tees off from the first tee.

Texas wedge: A shot played with a putter from just off the putting green.

Through the green: The whole area of the golf course except: (1) the teeing ground and putting green of the hole being played; (2) all hazards on the golf course.

Up: The number of holes a player is ahead. For example, three *up* and four holes to play in *match play*.

Up and down: Holing out in two strokes from off the green.

USGA: United States Golf Association, the governing body of golf in America. See also *R&A*.

Water hazard: Any sea, lake, pond, river, canal, ditch, or other open water within the confines of the course. These water hazards are marked by yellow stakes or yellow lines, and lateral hazards are marked with red stakes or lines.

Whiff: See *fresh air*.

Winter rules: Special rules set by the local golf club committee when a golf course is not in perfect condition. The golfer may improve the lie of the ball up to 6 inches in the fairway between the teeing ground and the green. These are only local rules, not USGA rules.

Wood: A typical set of woods (now usually made of metal) is numbered from 1 to 5. As the numbers go up, the loft on the club face increases and the shafts get shorter.

Resources

Associations and Organizations

Alliance of Youth Sports Organizations (AYSO)
P.O. Box 351
South Plainfield NJ 07080
E-mail: info@aoyso.com
AYSO organizes sports programs for young people.

American Junior Golf Association (AJGA)
1980 Sports Club Dr.
Braselton GA 30517
877-373-2542; 770-868-4200
E-mail: ajga@ajga.org
www.ajga.org/
Competitive junior golf.

International Foundation for Junior Golf (IFJG)
10688 Haddington
Houston TX 77094
832-358-8300
Fax 832-358-8383
E-mail: ifjg@ifjg.org
www.ifjg.org/
IFJG is an international non-profit with a Greens to Gowns program.

International Junior Golf Tour (IJGT)
P.O. Box 5130
Hilton Head Island SC 29938
843-785-2444
Fax 843-785-6199
E-mail: info@ijgt.com
www.ijgt.com/
Runs a series of 27 tournaments from September through May.

Ladies Professional Golf Association (LPGA) Junior Golfer
100 International Golf Dr.
Daytona Beach FL 32124
904-274-6200
Fax 904-274-1099
E-mail: tcp@fans.lpga.com
www.lpga.com/kids/
Offers a variety of programs, from scholarships to clinics.

National Amputee Golf Association (NAGA)
11 Walnut Hill Rd.
Amherst NH 03031
800-633-NAGA (800-633-6242)
E-mail: b1naga@aol.com
www.amputee-golf.org/
This nonprofit offers physical and mental therapy to amputees through involvement with golf. No annual dues for junior membership.

National Association of Golf Coaches and Educators (NAGCE)
7458 Somerset Shores Ct.
Orlando FL 32819
888-GO NAGCE (888-466-2423)
Fax 407-354-1295
E-mail: nagce@mindspring.com
www.nagce.org/
NAGCE's motto is "training those who impact golf's future."

National Association of Junior Golfers (NAJG)
11891 U.S. Hwy. 1, Suite 101
North Palm Beach FL 33408
561-691-3871
E-mail: info@najg.org
www.najg.org/
Junior golf information for parents,

kids, program administrators, and the golf industry.

National Minority Golf Foundation (NMGF)

7226 N. 16th St.
Phoenix AZ 85020
602-943-8399
Fax 602-943-8553
www.nmgf.org/jrgolfframe.htm
A resource bank of information on golf-related programs, projects, and scholarships for minorities. One of its goals is to involve more minority youth in the game of golf at an early age.

National Youth Sports Safety Foundation (NYSSF)

333 Longwood Avenue, Suite 202
Boston MA 02115
617-277-1171
Fax 617-277-2278
E-mail: nyssf@aol.com
www.nyssf.org/
NYSSF is a nonprofit, educational organization whose goal is to reduce the risks of sports injury to young people.

Parents Association for Youth Sports (PAYS)

2050 Vista Parkway
West Palm Beach FL 33411
800-729-2057; 800-688-KIDS (800-688-5437); 561-684-1141
Fax 561-684-2546
E-mail: nays@nays.org
www.nays.org/
Provides materials and information for youth sports programs to help

teach parents about their roles and responsibilities in children's sports activities.

Professional Golf Association of America (PGA of America)

100 Ave. of the Champions
Palm Beach Gardens FL 33410
561-624-8400
Fax 561-624-8452
www.pga.com/juniors/
Not related to the PGA Tour, this organization is a good source of information for teaching pros.

United States Blind Golf Association (USBGA)

c/o Bob Andrews, President
3094 Shamrock St. N.
Tallahassee FL 32308
850-893-4511
Fax 850-893-4511
E-mail: usbga@blindgolf.com
www.blindgolf.com/united_states/
u_s_home_page.htm
A nonprofit association that instructs coaches how to gauge distances, place a club head behind a ball, and encourage blind golfers to develop their abilities.

United States Golf Association (USGA)

P.O. Box 746
Far Hills NJ 07931
800-223-0041; 908-234-2300
Fax 908-234-9687
E-mail: usga@usga.org
www.usga.org/
Provides handicap index information and listings of state and local golf associations. Annually publishes the *Rules of Golf* and *Snoopy and Friends* (a rules book for children).

World Golf Hall of Fame
21 World Golf Place
St. Augustine FL 32092
904-940-4123
Fax 904-940-4374
www.wgv.com/wgvf_halloffame.html
Information on the game's greatest
players and contributors and their
accomplishments.

**Young Golfers of America
Association
(YGAA)**
4701 Keniston Ave.
Los Angeles CA 90043
323-292-7030
Fax 323-292-7099
E-mail: ygaa@pacbell.net
www.ygaa.com/
Programs that encourage youth to
participate in golf.

Programs

**American Sport Education
Program
(ASEP)**
P.O. Box 5076
Champaign IL 61825
800-747-5698
Fax 217-351-2674
E-mail: asep@hkusa.com
www.asep.com/
Instructional resources, workshops,
and courses for coaches, administra-
tors, and parents.

First Tee
World Golf Village
425 S. Legacy Trail
St. Augustine FL 32092
904-940-4300
www.thefirsttee.org
Provides affordable access to golf,

particularly for kids who might
otherwise not have an opportunity
to experience the game.

Hook a Kid on Golf
2050 Vista Parkway
West Palm Beach FL 33411
800-729-2057; 800-688-KIDS (800-
688-5437); 561-684-1141
Fax 561-684-2546
E-mail: hakog@nays.org
www.nays.org/
A comprehensive youth golf program designed for recreation agen-
cies or golf courses, sponsoring
introductory clinics, on-course
training programs, and golf leagues.

**Junior Golf and Academics of
America**
5850 Belvedere Rd., Suite 200
West Palm Beach FL 33413
561-640-3600; 561-697-8487
Fax 561-683-1618
E-mail: jgaainc@aol.com
www.jrglf.com/
The program teaches at-risk children the game of golf and increases
their academic skills performances.

Kids Golf: Drive, Pitch & Putt
P.O. Box 30098
Palm Beach Gardens FL 33420
561-691-1700
Fax 561-691-1894
E-mail: marketing@kidsgolf.com
www.kidsgolf.com/
The Drive, Pitch & Putt program
helps parents, kids, and golf directors by offering kids a fun and easy
way to enjoy golf.

LPGA Girls Golf Club (GGC)
100 International Golf Dr.

Daytona Beach FL 32124
904-274-6200
Fax 904-274-1099
E-mail: ggo@fans.lpga.com
www.lpga.com/kids/index.cfm?cont
   _id=38875
Introductory golf programs (instruction, on-course playing) for girls
ages 7 to 17 at 70+ sites across the
country.

Take Your Daughter to the Golf Course Week

National Golf Course Owners
   Association
1470 Ben Sawyer Blvd., Suite 18
Mt. Pleasant SC 29464
800-933-4262
Fax 843-881-9958
E-mail: info@ngcoa.org
www.getlinkedplaygolf.com/text/
   daughter.html
Annual event held each spring with
the goal of getting parents to introduce their daughters to golf.

Web Sites and Electronic Newsletters

Adapted Physical Education

E-mail: pec@pecentral.org
http://pe.central.vt.edu/adapted/
   adaptedmenu.html
This section of PE Central (see
below) offers information to help
teachers of physically challenged
students. The site suggests ways to
modify sports and activities to make
them accessible to all students.

Coaching Youth Sports

E-mail: rstratto@vt.edu
www.tandl.vt.edu/rstratto/CYS/
Virginia Tech's Health and Physical

Education program sponsors this
Web site, which provides coaches,
athletes, and parents with general,
rather than sport-specific, information about skills for youth. The site
also allows browsers to submit
questions.

golfsupport.com

www.golfsupport.com/
Offers golf tips and helps locate a
golf or teaching professional.

juniorgolf.com

www.juniorgolf.com/
Information for the junior golf com-
munity and their parents.

JuniorGolf News.com

www.juniorgolfnews.com/
News about junior golf events
around the world.

JuniorGolf Tournaments.com

E-mail: info@
   juniorgolftournaments.com
www.juniorgolftournaments.com/
Information about junior golf programs and junior golf tournaments
in the United States at the national,
state, and local level.

Linkaway Golf

www.linkaway.com/
Directory of 3,633 golf links from
107 countries.

National Junior Golf Scoreboard

E-mail: njgs@mindspring.com
www.njgs.com/
Recruiting resource for coaches, a
resource for junior golfers' parents,
and an events board for tournament
directors.

PE Central
E-mail: pec@pecentral.org
http://pe.central.vt.edu/
Information for physical education teachers, students, and parents on appropriate physical education programs, helping young people on their way to a lifetime of physical fitness and health.

Teaching Kids Golf
www.teachkidsgolf.com/
Free Kids Golf lessons with streaming video show kids and junior golfers (ages 2 to 12 years old) how to play golf and develop golf skills.

U.S. Kids Golf
www.uskidsgolf.com/
Encourages family interaction.

World of Sports.com: Youth Sports on the World Wide Web
www.worldofsports.com/
Coaches forum and relevant links.

General

The Golf Channel
7580 Commerce Center Dr.
Orlando FL 32819
407-345-4653
www.thegolfchannel.com/
For those who can't get enough: golf 24 hour a day, including instruction, pro tour coverage, and player profiles.

Lessons

To find a qualified teaching professional in your area, call the LPGA at 904-274-6200 or go to www.lpga.com and click on Teaching & Club Pros for a listing of instructors by region. Or, call the PGA or go to www.pga.com and click on Learning Center, then Pro Central.

Consult *The Guide to Golf Schools and Camps* (Shaw Guides, Inc., P.O. Box 231295, New York NY 10023, 212-799-6464, http://golf.shawguides.com/).

Index

Acknowledgments

A great big thanks to my parents, family, friends, and all the very special people in my life. I would like to thank each one of you. Thanks also to all the teachers and students who have touched my life over the last 30 years, particularly the juniors I currently work with. Thanks to all of you who spent many hours in the 100-degree heat without a complaint during the photo shoot for this book. I would especially like to thank my fellow professionals of the LPGA and the PGA, for sharing their knowledge of the game and teaching me so much. My teaching style has evolved by learning from many master teachers and mentors who willingly shared their knowledge and enthusiasm. I have taken the best of what other educators say and do and given it my own style and the benefit of my own personal experience.

Thanks to Tom McCarthy, Sandra Eriksson, Beth Daniel, Karrie Webb, Ita Butler, Darren Clarke, Colm Smith, Paulette Burrhus, Alan Pearson, and the staff of the Beaumont Country Club for their support. And finally, thanks to America for providing me with so many opportunities since I came to this great country.

About the Author

An LPGA Class A Teaching Professional, Detty Moore is a tenured assistant professor in the Health and Kinesiology Department at Lamar University in Beaumont, Texas. She has a longstanding involvement in golf education, with 30 years' teaching experience at the high school and college levels. She has taught in Ireland, Australia, and the United States and has coached high school and state teams in numerous sports.

As an LPGA Class A Teaching Professional, Detty has conducted golf academies and junior clinics in Ireland and the United States. She is currently on the teaching staff of Peggy Kirk Bell's Golfari, a golf school at Pine Needles, Southern Pines, North Carolina. Detty is director of the LPGA Girls Golf Club of Southeast Texas and works with many junior boys and girls in the region. In 1984–85, she was fitness advisor to Ireland's men's and women's golf teams, whose members went on to play the Curtis Cup, Walker Cup, the European Tour, and the PGA Tour.

Detty grew up in Kilkenny, Ireland, and came to the United States in 1987. She was nominated by *Golf for Women* magazine as one of the top 50 women golf teachers in the United States. She has received the Teaching Excellence Award at Lamar University on numerous occasions and is also the author of *Winning Edge Series: Golf* (McGraw-Hill).